CIRCLING
the
WAGONS

SECOND EDITION

When hiding a family secret, becomes more important than a loved one.

Written by Deborah Aldrick
Illustrations by Mitchell Aldrick

Copyright © Deborah Aldrick 2025

ALL RIGHTS RESERVED. No part of this book may be reproduced or transmitted in any form whatsoever, electronic, or mechanical, including photocopying, recording, or by any informational storage or retrieval system without the expressed written permission from the author and publisher.

Author: Deborah Aldrick
Title: Circling The Wagons – Second Edition
ISBN Paperback: 978-0-9756503-3-2
ISBN Kindle: 978-0-9756503-4-9

 A catalogue record for this book is available from the National Library of Australia.

Category: Survivor story/Family Relationships/Memoir/Autobiography
Publisher: Deborah Aldrick
Website/contact – www.dragonflyadvocacy.com.au

First Edition - published 2024

All insights offered are the authors own and are not intended to offend or replace any spiritual beliefs readers may hold. The author respects faith in its many expressions and encourages readers to follow their own beliefs.

LIMITS OF LIABILITY/ DISCLAIMER OF WARRANTY

The author and publisher of this book have used their best efforts in preparing this material and they disclaim any warranties, (expressed or implied) for any particular purpose. The information presented in this publication is compiled from sources believed to be accurate at the time of printing, however the publisher assumes no responsibility for omissions or errors. The author and publisher shall not be held liable for any loss or other damages, including, but not limited to incidental, consequential, or any other. This publication is not intended to replace or substitute medical or professional advice, the author and publisher disclaim any liability, loss or risk incurred as a direct or indirect consequence of the use of any content.

Contents

Dedication	5
Foreword	7
CHAPTER 1: Circling the wagons and what this means for family secrets	9
CHAPTER 2: Putting out fire with gasoline	13
CHAPTER 3: The people who have been abused are the experts	17
CHAPTER 4: Consent or the lack thereof	21
CHAPTER 5: The tree remembers what the axe forgets	27
CHAPTER 6: It's not your secret	33
CHAPTER 7: Telling your truth	37
CHAPTER 8: Destroyed my sense of safety	41
CHAPTER 9: The snow globe effect	47
CHAPTER 10: Broken branches of your family tree	55
CHAPTER 11: What's your moral worth	59
CHAPTER 12: The ongoing hurt	63
CHAPTER 13: Stand by me	71
CHAPTER 14: Fire collects all that it breathes	75
CHAPTER 15: The invisible perpetrator and the million-dollar question	81
CHAPTER 16: Grooming - it's not for animals	85
CHAPTER 17: The Confusion Within	93
CHAPTER 18: Who am I......really?	99
CHAPTER 19: Everybody's childhood plays itself out	107
CHAPTER 20: Trauma-induced emotional immaturity vs Bystander emotional immaturity	109
CHAPTER 21: Generational abuse	115
CHAPTER 22: Be a good CHAP	125
CHAPTER 23: Trauma Bonding	131

CHAPTER 24: Can't get off the roundabout — 141

CHAPTER 25: No good deed goes unpunished — 145

CHAPTER 26: Chop down your family tree — 149

CHAPTER 27: Eyes wide shut — 159

CHAPTER 28: Plants - an Analogy — 165

CHAPTER 29: Kaleidoscope — 169

CHAPTER 30: Age is no defence — 173

CHAPTER 31: They used our love against us — 177

CHAPTER 32: You can bid the mob good day — 183

CHAPTER 33: The only way out is through — 189

CHAPTER 34: You've always had the power, my dear...... — 201

CHAPTER 35: Give me your hand, so I can push you back down — 205

Acknowledgements — *211*

Testimonials — *213*

Author Bio — *217*

Glossary — *219*

Dedication

I dedicate this book to all the silenced generations, before me.

To all who have had their pain hidden and lived their lives in shame, a shame they did not deserve to feel.

To every little girl or boy who didn't understand why love had to hurt.

To every woman or man who struggled through the confusion of who their family members really were to them.

I also dedicate this book to Lenny (my dad) who didn't know until it was too late.

But selfishly, I also dedicate this book to the little girl inside me. The girl who deserved to be and have so much more in life. The girl who needed protection, but instead got silence and secrets.

Foreword

Circling The Wagons is a firsthand account of a survivor's struggles to reclaim her life after dealing with childhood abuse trauma hidden within a family environment.

This book is written for other survivors or family/friends of survivors. To get a true, in-depth, heartbreakingly raw and honest look into the devastating effects hidden childhood sexual abuse trauma can have when it is not dealt with for decades and to understand the process survivors go through in their journey to heal.

This book is not intended to take away from other survivors' accounts, needs and treatments. But to add an extra level of understanding and compassion from someone who has lived through similar circumstances of abuse.

The author wishes to show the reader how they may improve their circumstances through guidance, care and understanding, from a very grassroots level of writing.

There are thought-provoking and learning experiences written throughout this book. These examples are to guide survivors through their journey rather than to confront the reader.

Poems written from the heart throughout this book will show the strong emotional turmoil the author has grappled with and that other survivors may relate to.

Chapter 1

Circling the wagons and what this means for family secrets

Where to begin?

Maybe explaining the name of this book is the best place.

During the 1800s, many settlers travelled west from the East Coast of America in horse-drawn covered wagons. When the settlers would stop overnight or if threatened during the day they would line up their wagons in a circle, so they could best protect themselves from attack.

How does this title relate to my book? Well, throughout my book, I will show you how "circling the wagons" can have many different meanings and outcomes in the life of a childhood sexual abuse survivor. A child who has been abused in a family environment.

In life, we all find people there to help us or hurt us. (Givers or takers). Sometimes, throughout our lives, it is hard to decipher who is who. But when we are little, we look to our family as people who are there to nurture, help and support us. Our protectors. But what if some of these people are not who they seem?

Who am I? In terms of abuse and trauma, I am you or someone you know. Even if you don't think you know anyone who has suffered childhood sexual abuse, particularly in a family setting, you will because we are everywhere.

I grew up in the 70's & 80's on the northern beaches of Sydney, Australia. I have always thought of myself as nobody of much importance. Throughout my life, I have had such low self-esteem that I felt I wasn't smart enough, worthy enough, or important enough, and I tended to base my opinion of myself, on what I felt others thought of me. This was all due to my childhood abuse and the absence of help from my family. When you are made to feel like you are not worthy, or you are negatively controlled from such a young age it can become inbuilt into your everyday life.

My perpetrator was a family member. I will not give them oxygen by naming them; that is not why I am writing this book. I am writing for the sole purpose of helping others like myself to navigate life after abuse and trauma. You will find me posing and pondering on a lot of questions throughout this book. This is because child abuse and the trauma that follows is so complex and confusing, and I'm not sure anyone really has a full take on how this affects people. We all react and behave in different ways depending on our personalities, the degree and duration of the assault against us, and the extent of help we received, if any, after our abuse.

Intra-familial sexual abuse (child sexual abuse that occurs within a family environment) is said to be the most toxic and debilitating form of abuse that can be put upon a child by another family member. The trauma never really leaves them and most of the time they must be around the person who abused them, as they are part of their family. So, they are traumatised again and again throughout their life.

When someone is sexually abused/assaulted by a non-family member, they can stay away from their abuser most of the time. But when their abuser was a family member, that's usually not possible.

And this happens more than any of us are aware of because it is hidden within families. I call it the **"sick silence"** or the **"sick secret."** I am only one person, and besides myself, I know of so many others, be it family members or friends, who have experienced intra-familial sexual abuse.

An article I saw recently via a social media post talked about a detective who was investigating a child sexual assault case, which turned out to be in an intra-familial setting. During his time as a detective, he often found this type of assault happening in families but rarely were reports filed or charges laid. This is due to the family environment the abuse occurred within and the adult family members not following through to help the victim.

If a non-family member abused a child, we all hear of the outrage and assistance that is offered to the victim. Then, we hear of the follow-up repercussions to the perpetrator. But this rarely happens if a family member has committed the crime. And it is a crime! I feel the need to explain that because it is so often swept under the rug because other family members can't deal with the situation due to it being another family member who was the abuser/perpetrator/paedophile. So, therefore no action is taken.

This causes lifelong trauma and hurt to the victim. Just the fact that they are not helped and told to forget it is enough to send them spiralling down into a kind of "rabbit hole." This begins a life of self-doubt, low self-esteem, self-harm, obsessive behaviours, addiction, and the list goes on and on. Which I will look at in more detail later.

Childhood sexual abuse trauma doesn't just go away. But there are ways you can help yourself or others, and this is the purpose of my book. To help those who feel there is no hope or are still "eating shit politely" at the "table of denial" with their abuser or bystanders still in their lives.

This abuse happened to us, so we should be able to talk openly about our experiences and receive help. Yet we are told to keep quiet due to the family environment our abuse happened within. **How will we ever find the strength to move forward if we are once again controlled and muted in our later lives?** And what other past family secrets are we not aware of?

I don't want what I went through to be for nothing. Not if my experiences and understanding of this cycle can help others move forward in their own lives.

Not all the topics in this book are directly about my abuse, and I don't give graphic details on the acts themselves. There are lots of examples similar to other people's circumstances of abuse that I have seen or heard about throughout my life that I am bringing to light as a teaching tool.

This book should be used as a guide only. Guide meaning – to show or indicate the way to someone. I'll be on the journey with you, as a guide would, and this will be a long trek. **But the journey is important; the destination is waiting for you and it's your time now!**

Like the Lorax from Dr Seuss says – "I speak for the trees."

Well, in this book, "I speak for the Survivors." Until they can speak for themselves.

This book is also written for friends or family members of the adult survivor who are not equipped with the right education, information or techniques to help their loved ones.

From someone who has been there. As I get it, I've seen it, I know it, and I've lived it.

I believe the only way out - is through.

Chapter 2
Putting out fire with gasoline

The mind replays, what the heart can't forget.

David Bowie wrote a song in 1982 called "Putting Out Fire with Gasoline". As we all know, putting gasoline on a fire makes it burn dangerously and out of control. This is how some of us continue to live our lives and hurt ourselves after our abuse. Not because we want to but because it is a trauma response.

As briefly mentioned in Chapter 1 behaviours such as self-doubt, low self-esteem, self-harm, obsessive behaviours, addiction etc., are all manifested from childhood sexual abuse, and these can translate into lifelong psychological damage and consequences. This leads to educational difficulties, depression, and trouble forming and maintaining relationships later in life.

Let's look at self-doubt. What this looks like is never being sure of yourself or your choices. Running thoughts through your head a hundred times. Overthinking every move you make and still being unsure you made the right decision. Being a people pleaser and trying to make sure everyone else is happy. Never being your top priority in life, and because you doubt yourself, you can easily let the negative thoughts take over.

Low self-esteem leads to making bad or harmful choices. From the partners we choose, the jobs we take, the clothes we wear, and the people we surround ourselves with. The attention we sometimes seek from others, to make ourselves feel better in the short term. Accepting less than we deserve and letting others take advantage of us. And why wouldn't we let others take advantage of us when our own family members did?

Self-harm comes in when we feel like we need to take the pain out of our heads and attack our bodies instead. This kind of release feels good in the moment but does more harm in the long run as it really doesn't fix anything, and the judgement from others can make us feel even worse. So, the downward cycle continues. Things like anorexia, bulimia, binge eating, OCD, cutting, etc., are all ways people who have been abused will try to control their environment in some way. Which again results in more harm to themselves. Even gym junkies. People who you think are healthy can hide their pain by working out constantly. There's a reason they call them gym "junkies" and it's because they get addicted to working out and think their body image on the outside will take away from how they feel on the inside. I know it did for me in the past.

Addiction becomes another form of temporary relief from our trauma/pain. Whether it be alcohol, drugs, plastic surgery, gambling, steroids, sex, etc.. Once again, short-term release, long-term misery and this tears families apart.

Obsessive behaviours. There is a widely recognised connection between trauma and obsessive behaviours. OCD (Obsessive compulsive disorder).

Overworking. Not being able to stop and relax is also a way people try to keep themselves from thinking about what happened. Never slowing down temporarily helps you from dealing with your trauma. You can try not to give it time to raise its ugly head, but it always will at some point because you can't outrun yourself.

So, in a nutshell, we end up using unhealthy behaviours to cope with our past abuse.

Unhealed trauma manifests as

Fixing others
People pleasing
Co-dependency
Living on high alert
Fear of abandonment
Constant need for validation
Tolerating abusive behaviour
Difficulty setting boundaries
Attracting narcissistic partners
De-prioritising own needs

Chapter 3

The people who have been abused are the experts

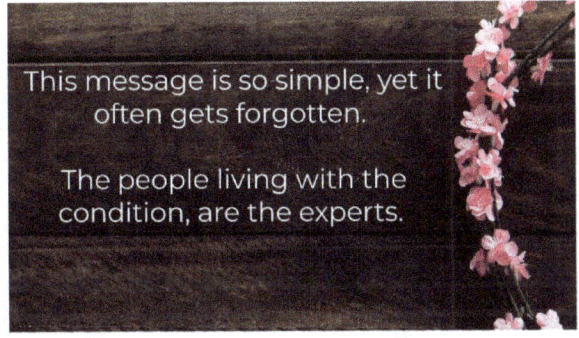

> This message is so simple, yet it often gets forgotten.
>
> The people living with the condition, are the experts.

I saw this message on social media. It stood out to me at the time, and I thought it would be a very important point to make, as it also relates to people who have been abused.

I am not saying psychologists, psychiatrists, counsellors etc., aren't the experts. Obviously, they've had the best training. They play a huge part in survivors' understanding and receiving the help and guidance they all need. I would never take away from that. What I do agree with is if you haven't experienced abuse firsthand, particularly in a family environment, you can't truly understand how someone feels at their very core. Survivors have lived with all the consequences that come from abuse over a lifetime. Day and night, and they don't get to knock off from it at the end of the day. It is there constantly for survivors throughout their lives. Everybody's experience is so different too, which makes it impossible for anyone to know just what a survivor has gone through to cope with their pain. This is another reason I wanted to write this book and write it in terms anyone can understand. No big words, scientific names or long, drawn-out explanations. I use plenty of examples throughout my book to try to make particular circumstances a lot more relatable and I know there are plenty of technical books out there already.

I have been abused in a family environment, and I have lived with all the consequences and repercussions that go hand in hand with this. Including the mental torture while trying to understand and find my way through life. With a lot of self-doubt and manipulation at times.

I can't unsee, unhear or unknow the abuse that the women in my circle, including myself, have been through.

So, this is my story and the knowledge I have acquired along the way. **I feel many other survivors will connect with or see parts of their own journey in my writing.**

To try to explain how I've come to understand abuse and trauma without traditional education pathways. I loosely relate my knowledge and experience to people like the "Indigenous peoples of the world" for example, due to the way they went about learning and helping each other. They use their life experiences, knowledge and wisdom they have acquired from watching and learning from their people, animals and nature. They would look to the wise Elders of the tribe to teach and mentor the younger generations.

They have also learnt not to make the same mistakes that their Elders have made. There was no university for them to attend back then. It was all life lessons. I have watched and listened carefully and, in turn, learnt from "my circle of friends and family." Including the mistakes, I have seen made in my past generations.

Also, people have approached me because they know what I've been through and feel safe talking to me about their lifelong struggles. **Hence, I have identified a pattern forming around these kinds of family abuse circumstances. That is what has led me to the title of this book – Circling The Wagons.**

Who else but the people who have lived through childhood sexual abuse can explain to you what it feels like to be dominated, manipulated, and ultimately controlled by someone they considered to be a loved one? To trust someone completely and have them use their power over you, against you. To go to bed at night, close your eyes and hide under the covers with your heart racing. Hoping they wouldn't come into your room that night.

Or to wake with a start when you feel them slipping under the covers next to you and hold your breath and try to be invisible until they are finished? To feel totally humiliated when they use coercive control over you, to keep you down. Then the shame you come to feel when you realise, as you get older, exactly what terrible acts transpired.

I have been to many sessions with psychologists to help me get to where I am now with the understanding of how abuse and trauma all play out in people's lives. So, I feel I have lived experience and knowledge in this area and a lot of self-discovery and healing over the years. I have personally seen how this type of intra-familial abuse can affect more than one generation of families, with the tentacles that reach far and wide. I have seen whole families torn apart by one person's self-satisfying, sick actions and the ramifications of the silence and secrets kept within families.

I wish I had someone who could guide me and help me to understand my own abuse. To explain why I felt the way I did when I was in my teens and 20s, and first trying to process all that had happened to me. If I can help just one person to better understand and move forward before they are middle-aged, when this seems to all blow up the most if they haven't yet dealt with their abuse. Then I will feel my life has meant something. A kind of purpose I have looked for, for a long time. **I want others to have the life they should have had, not what they have settled for or think is all they deserve due to their inaccurate, low opinion of themselves.**

I have heard of so many men and women around forty who suddenly start to change, due to them not being able to push their pain and trauma down any longer and finally wanting answers. Their families won't understand the sudden dark change in their loved ones. From drinking more, depression, crying, angry outbursts, substance abuse, violence and sadly sometimes suicide. Particularly with men. Divorce or separation is often the outcome of pulling away from family and friends. Sometimes, the real cause is never really known, as the childhood abuse survivor won't or can't speak of their abuse as they feel too guilty, scared or ashamed. This leads to my chapter further on – **"It's not your secret!"**

Chapter 4

Consent or the lack thereof

There is no such thing as getting consent from a child.

Children do not have the intellectual or emotional capacity to give consent for an adult or another child to touch them in a sexual manner.

Any kind of sexual contact with a child should be called rape. That's the way I see it, plain and simple. This may not be everyone's definition. But to me, if an adult makes a child do something sexual for their own gratification and sick pleasure against the child's wishes or ability to understand, then what other word is there to use?

Rape is a type of sexual assault carried out against a person without their consent. The act may be carried out by physical force, coercion, abuse of authority, or against a person who is incapable of giving valid consent. Such as one who is unconscious, incapacitated, has an intellectual disability or is below the legal age of consent – such as a child.

There are terms for someone taking something from someone else without their permission or consent. Such as if someone steals a handbag. It's called theft, not luggage abuse. So why isn't any kind of sexual contact with children called rape instead of sexual abuse? The term sexual abuse does not seem harsh enough for the crime. You can get your handbag back, unlike the crime against a child. Once that's committed, there is no getting their innocence or the detriment of their mental health back.

Children are trusting by nature. They are innocent and don't realise what sexual contact is or means. When you are a kid, you just accept what is.

Only the lowest of low indulge in sexual contact with a child. These are the kind of people who take advantage of a child's age, weakness, and vulnerability and it was unnatural what our family members did to us. They are cowards and perverts and the lowest form of humans. Even though my abuser was not an adult, they still knew how to manipulate me as I was vulnerable and had a very easy-going, willing-to-please kind of nature as a little girl. It all seemed like a game to me at first. But as the years went by and I tried to stop them, they would use coercive control to manipulate, threaten or blackmail me to keep their secret, which allowed them to continue their sick acts.

I know what they did. They know what they did. But I don't feel the need to include the particular details in this book. I am sure there are instances I have blocked out as well. The coercive control they had over me from such a young age is probably just as bad as the sexual component. Influencing my thoughts and behaviour and, in turn, making me into a child who didn't know her own mind, would be easily led, made to feel shame and guilt and wouldn't take her own paths in life. I was told that when I was a little girl, I followed them around like a little puppy dog, doing whatever they said! That's a very telling statement.

How manipulation works –

- The first stage of manipulation begins with the perpetrator putting on a façade of being kind, caring and helpful: persistent excessive attention, love and flattery.
- Isolation – when the person who manipulates you starts to isolate you from your friends or family and does things to you in private.
- Devaluing you, making you feel small, stupid, ashamed, unsure, etc..
- Fear or violence; making you feel scared or obligated to do something that feels wrong and ultimately, you feel fear of saying anything to anyone else due to your shame.

Broken promises

Down I came, one winter's day,
A little girl with eyes so brown,
A friend for you, with whom to play,
Sitting together watching Charlie Brown.

God made a deal and had you sign,
Said, she's part of your family now,
He only asked that you be kind,
You said you would and made a vow.

So, He left me there and went back home,
So many more angels to deliver,
But He would have kept me, had He known,
That you would drag me down that river.

What you stole, you can't give back,
And broken promises weren't all,
How many times, I just lost track,
How could I fight, I was so small.

You didn't think to read the terms,
The contract said you are to protect,
The older one should do no harm,
Your words and actions don't reflect.

So many things you stole from me,
Firstly, it was my innocence,
My childhood and my sense of safety,
Not to mention my first kiss.

God will come back down one day,
He'll ask you why and want the proof,
So, figure out what you're going to say,
And by the way, He knows the truth!

Chapter 5

The tree remembers what the axe forgets

I wish I could say I wrote this saying, as it sums up sexual abuse perfectly.

The tree – being the victim.
The Axe – being the perpetrator.

What affects us deeply and profoundly is written on our souls, and trauma from our abuse remains with us, whether we like it or not.

Dark and hurtful things that happened to you beyond your control when you were young are embedded deeply within you and have a way of popping their ugly heads up throughout your life.

It is like having a rubber ducky in the bath as a kid. You can push it under the water, but it always pops up again. Trauma that is not dealt with will have this exact effect. **If you do not deal with your mind, your body will find a way to do it for you.** In fact, you may go along with your life just fine for a long time. But as soon as things get hard, or your life takes a turn for the worse, or you get older and have not dealt with your abuse, it's there to take you to that dark place again. I personally know how this feels, as this has happened many times throughout my life, as explained in Chapter 27 – Eyes Wide Shut.

So, the tree (victim/survivor) remembers. But the Axe, (the perpetrator), who was not adversely affected during the encounter (often quite the contrary) does not have the same imprinted memory as the survivor may have.

This is why, so many survivors can have their day in court against their perpetrators, years or even decades after the offence took place, as the courts now take into consideration the exact details the survivor can remember. Even when asked time after time what happened, they can recall it exactly, as it is so clear to them because they were affected so greatly. Psychologists and psychiatrists will be able to tell from a survivor's raw reactions and trauma responses that what they are saying is true. This is a great outcome for people who have suffered deeply. To be heard and validated at last, and for their abusers to be punished finally.

Some of the things that survivors can remember are -

- Smell
- Taste
- Sounds
- Physical sensation
- Visual details

Smells – the survivor may remember an odour from their abuser when they come across it again. Things such as foul body odour, tobacco, alcohol, cologne, etc... One of mine was the smell of a toilet block.

This memory was triggered when I walked past my kids' school toilets when I became a parent.

I also remember a very foul, manly body odour from another family member. The memory of them is triggered when I walk past someone else who smells the same, at shops, etc... But I can't remember if they did anything to me. But I was scared of them as a small girl and would scream if they came near me. I have since found out they abused other children.

Tastes – a survivor may remember a strange or horrible taste from their abuse, even alcohol.

Sounds – a child may have heard the words - lie down, be quiet, don't move, this is our secret, you can't tell anyone, I'll hurt you or your family. Or even the words – "I love you," sadly! Or there may have been a TV show playing in the background or a particular song they heard at the time of their abuse. Can you imagine when you're an adult, having a future partner say – "I love you" during sex, and having this memory triggered? When it should be a nice thing to hear, but it makes your skin crawl.

Physical sensation/touch – being held down, cornered, a heavy force on them, pain, roughness, choking, etc., may be some of the things a survivor will remember if it happens to them later in life.

I have found it hard to be in a room I feel I can't leave, as I feel trapped. Even though logically I know I'm okay, it still triggers an anxious reaction in me.

This had become a huge trigger for me during my school days and later at college, especially during exams, due to the fact that you can't just walk out of a classroom anytime you like. Just this thought entering my mind would trigger a flight response, which usually leads to my IBS (irritable bowel syndrome – stomach cramps) being set off.

This, unfortunately, made it impossible for me to further my education back then. I would have liked to have been able to pursue a different profession when I was younger. Just one form of collateral damage from my abuse. As I've gotten older, I also struggle to be in elevators, in case I get locked in and trapped.

Visual details – A survivor may recall a room or even the wallpaper in a room, a person's face was red, the room was very dark, or there was more than one person. I remember being in a bath or shower during some of my abuse. Or it happened at my grandparents' place, in the toilet etc.

I can work out timelines of my abuse from memories of which house I was in. Or particular rooms in the house, and therefore, I can work out my approximate age at the time of my abuse.

These are all memories children may recall when they are adults and exposed to these images or sensations during their everyday lives. Until then, they may have repressed the memories, due to their mind not being able to cope with the distress and trauma.

When these painful memories are triggered, it will be very confronting and quite overwhelming to the survivor. It will take a toll on survivors, and they will need time to work through these memories. **But working through our trauma is an important step in healing.**

When we have repressed traumatic memories from childhood, we may experience symptoms associated with these memories into adulthood.

Things such as –

- Anxiety
- Mood swings
- Childish reactions
- Attachment issues

- Inability to cope with stress
- Low self-esteem
- Constantly on edge
- Chronic pain or illness

I can tick off at least 6 symptoms, and you will read more about my experiences.

Unhealed trauma can look like

Heightened fight or flight mode
Chronic fatigue or pain
Headaches
Stomach aches
Skin picking or hair pulling
Addictions
Autoimmune symptoms
Unprovoked anger/blacking out

Chapter 6

It's not your secret

This took me a long time to realise. It's not my secret. It's theirs!

It's actually my story, and stories are for telling, and most importantly, STORIES CAN SAVE LIVES!

As a child, I was scared to tell anyone what was going on for so long because I was told it was a secret and that I shouldn't tell. At first, I thought it was a game. But after a while, it started feeling yucky. (Yucky – kids word I know, but I was a kid). It made my skin crawl; the smell and touch of them was incredibly distressing to me. The problem was that they were not only sexually abusive but emotionally, mentally and, at times, physically abusive. They used coercive control over me by being nice when they wanted something (sucked me in). Then abusive when I refused them, which didn't happen very often due to my easily manipulated personality. This made me a very confused little girl who wasn't sure of anything anymore and didn't know right or wrong. My abuser was known as anti-social, highly strung, had anger issues, etc.. So, they got what they wanted, whether from me or others.

At times, we played tennis on the same team, and even if they made a mistake and lost a point, they would blame me and tell me it was my fault, as I shouldn't have hit the ball back the way I had, the shot before. They would throw their racquet and lose their temper and yell and humiliate me in front of other kids. The everyday things I did, were picked apart by this person. They made fun of me whenever they could. I remember driving with my Poppa on holidays and singing in the car when my abuser decided to tell me to shut up. My Poppa stood up for me and said, "She can sing if she wants!" But it was too late because I already felt put down, and the joy had been sucked out of the moment.

I was, for the most part, a happy little girl. I loved to jump on my trampoline, listen to the radio and sing. Or, at our 2nd house, go over the street to the local park and just swing on the swing for hours (singing again). Lol!

I just wanted peace, but what I got was anything but.

These may seem like small, insignificant points to make, but, it was just another part of the manipulation, coercive control and how they made me feel bad or stupid for something that was never my fault. This kind of manipulation was explained in more detail at the end of Chapter 4 - How manipulation works.

So, these kinds of examples show how we can be controlled, put down or feel we did something wrong when we didn't, and I'm sure others can relate to this scenario. I was just feeling my way through life back then as a young, impressionable girl, and this kind of treatment has had a huge impact on my developmental years. As a very small child, I looked up to them so much that I even write with my left hand, because they did. My teachers would take my pencil from my left hand and put it in my right hand, but I'd just switch it back while they weren't looking. I am right-handed at everything else I do.

Back to it's not your secret.......

When we are young, we take what adults, our peers, or people we feel are in control say as gospel.

They were our elders or someone we looked up to, and we were taught as kids to obey and respect these people. Especially kids who grew up in my generation, around the 1970's & 80's. Kids are generally very agreeable when told by an adult, older child or even a dominant peer to do something. Especially if they feel pressure or there is manipulation of any kind. To add to this, a bullying type of personality from their abuser would wear any kid down eventually, particularly if they had to live in the same house as their abuser. **Kids do what they need to survive from one day to the next. I know I did.**

Expecting consent from a child would be like getting an illiterate adult to sign something they can't read and trust the person who made them sign it. They are both clueless about what they are doing.

In cases of abuse, they still have that same hold over you. You just don't know at the time what they are doing to you, or making you do to them, is wrong. You may feel like you participated, so, therefore, you were complicit. This is not the case. As mentioned earlier, you did not have the intellectual or emotional capacity to know or give consent. They were grooming you and ultimately sexualising you.

BUT AT NO TIME WERE YOU RESPONSIBLE! This is the most important message I want to convey in this book! Because these thoughts have done us all the most damage!

So, let's get that clear right from the beginning.

I'm sure if we all had our time again and could put our (mature heads on our young shoulders), we would stand up for ourselves and tell someone about our abuser then and there and cop whatever punishment was given out at the time. Just so we didn't have to live the rest of our lives with the continual pain and our trauma responses to our memories of sexual abuse.

You have the right to tell whoever you want about your abuse.

They (your perpetrator) will try to make sure no one believes you. This is the biggest struggle you will come up against, and I speak more about that later in Chapter 15.

Chapter 7

Telling your truth

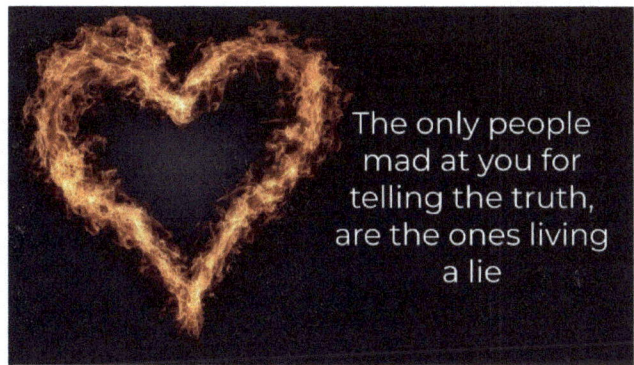

You are entitled to say what you went through and to tell anyone what happened to you. I realise this is a very hard thing to do. It may take you a long time to build up the courage to do so, especially if you have already tried at some point and were not believed or you were dismissed.

I told my supposed protector what was happening to me when I was a kid.

(You'll hear me talk a lot about my "supposed protector." They were the person who was supposed to protect me against my abuser but didn't, and I also refer to them as a bystander).

Very little was done back then, and the abuse continued for a while longer. In fact, just recently, I talked to my supposed protector about how the abuse continued because they did little to nothing when I first told them. The only thing they did back then was yell at my abuser when they caught them in my room one night. My supposed protector told me as an adult that "I" should have let them know the abuse was continuing.

It is quite uncommon for children to speak up at all about their abuse. Even once. To find the right way to explain to an adult what's happening. Because we can't understand ourselves as kids. Since little was done the first time I spoke up, and believe me, I copped it from my abuser for telling on them. How did my supposed protector expect me to find the strength to speak up again? By their inaction, I was shown that what was happening, was unimportant. So that's how I was made to feel about the whole situation. **That it wasn't that important.**

Parents should not expect their kids to find the right words or courage to speak about what's happening to them as they not only don't understand themselves, but they would be being coerced and manipulated to keep quiet also. That's why parents need to be proactive and ensure they have their eyes open and are looking for signs of changes in their children. Some of these changes I speak about in Chapter 27 – Eyes Wide Shut.

I tried to speak to my supposed protector about my abuse again in my early 20s. They listened in the car. I can tell you the exact place we were when I spoke to them because it was very distressing for me, and it took a lot of courage to bring it up again. So, the memory has stayed with me. Nothing was done in terms of holding my abuser accountable or even speaking to them about what took place. My supposed protector didn't "get it" once again. So, I went back to being the accommodating family member who didn't make a fuss.

I have seen many doctors and psychologists throughout my life, starting from my early 20s.

I told my long-term doctor about my abuse about five years after first seeing her when I was in my 30s. I remember her saying – "Oh Deb, that explains so much." **She could see so many signs of trauma in my behaviour, especially all my anxiety and over-protectiveness of my children.**

My doctor described my journey years later as peeling an onion, and she was right.

It happens in layers. You might get some direction or guidance from one professional, and later in life, you may get more help in another form until you finally feel like you are getting somewhere and becoming closer to the person you should have been. Because you have educated yourself about what happened and worked through your trauma, and are a healthier version of yourself.

When I was seeing a psychologist in my early 40s and continually struggling with having to be around my abuser at family gatherings, my psychologist said something in one of our sessions that changed my whole life for the better.

It was so simple, but I had never considered it to be an option for me in the past.

"You don't have to see your abuser; you know that, don't you, Deb?"

THAT SENTENCE CHANGED EVERYTHING FOR ME!

At first, I thought it would be impossible because I had always been the amenable one in our family. But then I started thinking. And it was around my abuser's birthday that I just couldn't bring myself to call them to wish them a happy birthday. I had asked my parents to let my abuser know why I wouldn't be calling after finally sitting my dad down to tell him what happened to me when I was little. Which I will explain in more detail later. I am not going to lie. It was a very hard time, and I had a lot of anxiety knowing I was about to blow up my whole family.

But it just had to be done. It was time.

I couldn't continue to push my feelings down and have this person in my life any longer. I am so thankful every day for my psychologist giving me this advice.

To an unabused person, pulling away from our family member who abused us may seem like a very simple step to take. But if you really think about all the repercussions of doing this in a family environment, you will understand why this is such a hard decision to make because it doesn't just affect you and your abuser. It has an impact on your whole family.

"How's your 'bleep' going, Deb?" When you run into an old friend.

Extended family asking, "Why isn't 'bleep' and their family at the Christmas gathering anymore?"

"Where did you grow up? What was your childhood like?" Questions from a new friend.

Or when your kids ask – "Why don't we see 'bleep' anymore?"

"Why can't you just forget what happened back then and see them?" From an ignorant family member. Etc. etc. etc.

Chapter 8
Destroyed my sense of safety

They knew what they were doing was wrong, because they did it in secret

Home was supposed to be a safe place when we were growing up. But for a lot of us, it wasn't.

We might not have known what was normal at the time. But as we grew older and saw friends' or partners' families operate differently from ours, we began to realise how we were living and being treated wasn't right or normal. I remember when I was about 14 or 15 years old, and realised for the first time, that what had happened to me WAS SEXUAL ABUSE! But I still couldn't process it.

Kids these days have a lot more access and knowledge about how to keep their private parts safe, but back when I was a kid, very little was talked about in this area.

The sad truth is that as a child, I didn't realise that I deserved to be treated better by this person. With kindness and respect - not control. I knew this was my reality and didn't question why I was being treated this way. I just put up with it, as I knew no better.

Child abuse doesn't always have to be sexual in nature either. It can be verbal, physical, emotional, coercive control, etc.. You might have been the easiest child to coerce, and not the strongest-willed. Therefore, you were manipulated, got less or were treated badly. Trauma can develop from this also, which can lead to family dysfunction in the future.

Look at Cinderella, for example. This shows a stepmother abusing her stepdaughter by making her their slave. Such an early example of coercive control.

The squeaky wheel gets the oil. This means the one who is the loudest, most demanding, highly emotional and manipulative will get all the attention and have the most control in the family.

It's not fair, but that's how family dynamics work at times, especially if your parents weren't the strongest-willed people and didn't discipline your siblings or hold their abusive spouses to account.

I feel that my abuser had very different morals from me as a kid. When I did stand up to them about the wrongs they were doing, I got punished. Therefore, this was another form of coercive control they used over me.

I remember a neighbour of ours, Isobel. She found what we called as kids a "wooden pear" growing in our local cul de sac, park, where we all played. It was closest to her house, and she had been waiting for it to grow. It was well known amongst the kids in our neighbourhood that it was Isobel's. But my abuser decided that they were going to steal it. She was so upset to find it gone. So, when I found out who took it, I told her. Oops!

My abuser was made to give it back to her, and I paid the price for telling. Most kids know what is right and wrong, and I speak about people's "Moral worth" in Chapter 11.

One of my psychologists told me that my abuser probably controlled our household from an early age due to how demanding they were. Even though it wasn't right, it was probably easier for my family members to give in to my abuser than deal with their moods and anger.

Which then made it much easier for my abuser to control me.

They would take advantage of me when they had me isolated. Such as when we were left with extended family on school holidays. Home alone after school when I was little or when people were sleeping. This shows me that they knew what they were doing was wrong. Because they did it in secret.

There are a lot of things that make so much more sense now that I've been able to put them into perspective. I remember the words they said and the timelines they did things. The instances of humiliation have actually made my memory of some of my abuse so much stronger and clearer. Without this humiliation, I may not have remembered certain events.

Between the abuse and silencing. What was done to us as victims of family abuse is a form of brainwashing.

Brainwashing – any technique designed to manipulate human thought or action against the desire, will or knowledge of the individual.

Even though I talk about how we've all reacted in our own ways and how our negative behaviours from our abuse have been so different, the feelings of hurt, confusion, anger and sadness that our abuse has brought about would all be very similar.

I didn't sleep well as a kid, and still don't sleep soundly. My abuser snuck into my room at times, so I wasn't able to get the deep sleep a child should have. I became highly alert from a young age and still wake at the slightest sound.

Shallow breathing can also be a sign of an adult who was abused as a child. We don't tend to relax easily or much at all compared to people who weren't abused. Our senses were heightened from a very young age, and that's how our breathing developed. In a later chapter, I speak about how meditation is so helpful with this.

My husband, for example, probably takes one breath compared to my 2 or 3 breaths. His head hits the pillow at night, and usually, he's out like a light. I take a lot longer to get to sleep, and it is certainly not sound.

Abuse can also happen later in life to adults. A person of any age who has been in a traumatic situation. Held against their will, felt a lack of control, domestic violence, raped or somehow physically or sexually assaulted. Will have similar trauma symptoms as childhood victims.

Too

I was too young, too naïve, too vulnerable, too impressionable.

There was too little supervision, too little control, too little understanding, too little help.

Then there was too much hurt, too much loss, too much devastation, too much suffering.

It was all just "too" much.

Chapter 9

The snow globe effect

Family abuse is different to outside abuse or (non-family) abuse. I relate it to being trapped in a snow globe.

You can't get out as a kid. Where are you going to go?

So, you are literally stuck in this tiny world of abuse that no one knows about but you and your perpetrator, and there is no easy escape! Even when a parent does find out.

Below are some examples of what intra-familial abuse can look like, when no one holds the perpetrator to account, and no help is forthcoming to the victim, from their family. These examples show how these acts are allowed to continue and why the victims will become the family scapegoats in the future.

Example 1 – Brother molests his sister back in the '70s

What does the parent do if they know about it?

Where can the brother be sent, even if they had money to send him somewhere? And if they send him to another family or boarding school, etc... Does he molest another child? Most probably because he's highly sexualised and has gotten away with it before.

Who will the parent tell? No one, because the subject is taboo.

So, the victim remains in the home with the brother, and the abuse continues, and the sister never feels protected or a priority.

Example 2 – Father molests daughter in the '80s

Mother finds out – what does she do?

There is no information out there to tell her how to handle this, and she won't speak about it to any friends, etc.. for fear of being judged.

Mother relies on her husband for his income, as a lot of wives didn't work in the 80's.

Mother tells her daughter not to say anything.

Daughter becomes rebellious in her teens, risk-taking, verbally abusive to parents, sexually active at a young age, teen pregnancy maybe?

She makes poor choices in partners/friends, pulls away from family as soon as she's able to and moves out.

Daughter, therefore, becomes the black sheep of the family – the "troubled one" the scapegoat, and the one the family chooses not to be around a lot.

The other siblings pull away from her also as they feel she doesn't treat their parents well due to them not knowing what happened to their sister.

Dad never pays the price for what he did, and Mum is complicit as a bystander.

Example 3 – Brother molests brother

Older brother grooms and makes his younger brother sexually active for his own pleasure.

Younger brother doesn't realise what's going on at the time.

Younger brother realises during his teenage years what has happened to him.

He hates his older brother and there are physical fights often and they can't stand being in the same room.

Older brother puts down and ostracises younger brother to try to keep his "sick secret".

Younger brother finally crumples and tells his mother.

Mother doesn't believe him and offers no help.

Younger brother becomes violent, risk-taking, takes drugs and is totally out of control.

Older brother becomes the favourite as he's the well-controlled son and becomes the golden child of the family. Goes on to have a good career, etc...

Younger brother gets into trouble with the law and does stints in jail, and his family looks down on him.

Younger brother starts to hate women in general due to his mother not believing or protecting him. He, therefore, becomes abusive towards future female partners.

Younger brother can't keep a job as his anger gets the better of him, and his life spirals from there. Unless he finally gets help.

Example 4 – Uncle molests nephew

Uncle starts to take an interest in his nephew. Takes him fishing, for drives, camping, etc..

Uncle is grooming nephew just like uncle's grandfather groomed him when he was young.

Nephew feels special at first by being singled out by his uncle.

Later, nephew starts acting up at home. He is only six years old and is usually a really good kid.

Nephew starts to wet his bed.

Nephew pretends to be sick when uncle is due to pick him up.

Eventually, mother realises her son is faking illness and makes him go with his uncle.

The abuse continues...........

Nephew, now a teenager, gets into a physical fight with uncle at a Christmas get-together.

Mother reprimands her son, and the extended family wonders what's gotten into nephew?

Uncle gets off scot-free.

This snow globe we were all trapped in was very real.

Some people may not understand why we couldn't get out. But due to the complete control we felt under (not to mention our age at the time of our abuse), we didn't have the power, strength, means or knowledge to escape.

Sexual abuse victims are able to physically walk out the door at any time, but their minds are held hostage!

Our children are the most important thing in this world and keeping them safe during their formative years is paramount. They will be the mothers and fathers, uncles, aunts and grandparents of the future, and if they do not have a good beginning in life, the next generation will suffer.

I am going to do a couple of little analogies here.

I am going to compare our families' unfair responses and silencing of us, to a person going to a Bike shop to buy a bike, and also trying to traverse the Great Wall of China.

The red bike.

You walk in and see a red bike you would like to buy at a bike shop. You go up to the counter and tell the owner that you would like to buy that red bike, in the window.

The owner says no, you cannot buy a bike from my shop.

But you say it is the perfect bike for me, the right colour, size, it has the basket on the front you've been looking for to carry your groceries from the shop. The bell works, it's perfect and you are willing to pay full price.

You ask if it is already sold and they say no, it's still for sale.

You then question why you can't buy it?

And the shop owner still says no but doesn't have a good reason.

You try again and even offer an extra $50 to buy that red bike.

Once again the shop owner won't budge and then they start to get angry with you and ask you to leave their shop. They tell you to go to the bike shop up the road, but you can't buy a bike from me.

So, you walk out of the shop and cannot understand why they have treated you this way.

In this story the shop owner is your family member, and the bike is your story, power and truth. They won't let you have it no matter what. No matter how hard you beg and plead and offer more. This bike will never be yours. You can go up the road and receive love, understanding and have someone listen and help you, but your family is not willing to give you this. They will sell that bike to someone who is not in the family, but they won't let go of that bike to you, ever. Because there are consequences around admittance, if they were to give it to you.

The great wall of China

Another analogy of intra-familial childhood abuse when the child grows older.

Talking about your abuse to your family, can at times be like trying to scale or get around the great wall of China.

You claw at the bricks to try to get a hand hold to climb it, as it looks to be the quickest way over. But it's just too flat and slippery and there's no way to get up it. So, you walk away and give up.

So many times, you return to that wall, and you look up and side to side, and you just can't see an end to it, no matter how far back you stand to try and see where it finishes. So once again you return home and give up and try to move on and not think about that wall.

But the thought of getting over that wall just won't leave your mind. You see friends who've made the trek and you know how well they are doing. You also know friends who've never had to scale that wall to be happy, and that feels so unfair to you. So, you go back home and feel sorry for yourself. Once again giving up on that wall.

Eventually you realise that you just have to make that journey, no matter how long it will take you to walk the length of that wall. It's the only way. You just can't stay where you are anymore, it's too painful to remain stuck there.

So, you start walking and walking and walking. At times you stop and sob and almost give up and turn back because that's what you've always done before. You think to yourself maybe it wasn't that bad where I was? But then you remember just how painful it really was back there and start on that trek again.

You get blisters on your feet, trip over fallen branches, freeze sleeping outside at night and hear the wild animals howling, which frightens you. But the further you travel away from where you were stuck, the brighter the sun appears, the warmer the nights become, and your feet get calluses to cover those blisters and stop hurting.

Finally, you see the end of the wall and feel this overwhelming sense of power and freedom come over you. And there you are, you have finally found the YOU, you have been looking for your whole life. And it's just magic.

Chapter 10
Broken branches of your family tree

Fingers pointing at everyone but the perpetrator.

I want to show you an example of a family tree where everyone is so busy looking at and hating on everyone else that no one is looking at the perpetrator. Which is exactly the way the perpetrator wants it because of the abuse being in a family setting and the silence that goes along with this. No one is holding the perpetrator to account, and this usually only happens in intra-familial abuse circumstances.

Father - James
Mother - Jenny
Daughter 1 - Sally
Daughter 2 - Fiona
Son – Angus

James grooms both Sally and Fiona from a fairly young age. Sally is the more dominant personality. So, James directs all his attention to Fiona instead, as she is a lot easier to manipulate. Fiona feels special because she has become Daddy's girl. He makes more fuss about her than anyone else in the family. Gives her special attention at first, but then it turns sexual.

Both Sally & Fiona develop eating disorders during their late teens/early twenties. Sally doesn't know what happened to Fiona or that it was much worse than what she had experienced. Fiona doesn't know if anything happened to Sally as they don't speak of it. The "sick silence."

Fiona becomes highly sexualised as a young adult, is risk-taking, picks bad partners throughout her life and becomes a teenage mum.

Sally becomes hardened in her attitude to life and shuts people out.

At some point, Fiona tells her mother, Jenny, what happened. Jenny yells angrily at Fiona, says she doesn't believe her and tells her not to talk about it again.

Jenny becomes guilt-ridden. She doesn't know what to do about her husband or daughter. She starts to drink heavily to numb the pain. At times she can block out what happened, but not forever.

Angus has no idea what's happened. But he can feel tension around his family and doesn't understand why Fiona and his parents fight so much.

Sally has left the family fold. She can't deal with them anymore and she becomes the centre of the family's negative attention because she's pulled away.

Guess who has gotten off once again without any punishment or shame! Yep, it's James, the perpetrator.

This is how "the wagons" come to circle the "wrong person." They are protecting the "secret" and in turn "the perpetrator" instead of the victim because they don't want anyone outside the family to find out about their shame and all the repercussions that would surely come about from holding the perpetrator to account. By the end of this book, I hope to show you how it should be, instead of how it is, and if your family continues to circle the wrong person **then you should find different wagons in your life.**

Chapter 11

What's your moral worth

Throughout life, we see people get away with things that are morally wrong. Maybe not legally wrong, but morally wrong.

Example - if you see money drop from someone's wallet and they don't realise? Do you pick it up and give it to them? Or do you wait, see if they don't notice, and take it yourself? That's what I mean by moral worth. There's a different scale for everyone. People who do good deeds because someone is watching. Compared to someone who does it no matter if they will be seen or congratulated. Down to the selfish people who are just out for themselves.

When I hear about a child/person who has been abused and find out their own family doesn't do anything to help them, no matter how old they are at the time their family finds out, that's morally wrong!

Why would their own family not help? Who could live with themselves knowing what their loved one has been through and not help? These are questions that baffle me. I just can't get my head around this kind of behaviour, and this happens all the time in these kinds of intra-familial sexual abuse instances.

One of the reasons it is so upsetting to me is that it has happened to me, too. Why did my supposed protector not protect me? How could they not if they loved me? As a child and now an adult, it is still so confusing and hurtful to think someone could display such low emotional intelligence. How could they not understand how the abuse you have been through isn't relevant enough for them to act on it? Even later in life. Or are they are so guilt-ridden that they block it out of their head or try to minimise the incidents? This is the question! **I also feel as though they didn't help me because helping would mean admitting to what happened to me.** And they didn't want to admit that to themselves or anyone else either.

The family connection between myself and my abuser is the reason my supposed protector didn't step up and help me. However, the family connection did not minimise the experience for me. It prolonged it and made my trauma so much worse because of the shame and so many other underlying feelings that intra-familial sexual abuse brings about.

I am still struggling to have a relationship with the person who was supposed to protect me. I haven't seen my abuser for over seven years now. But my supposed protector is still the conduit (connection) that keeps my trauma alive. When my supposed protector passes away, there will be no further connection. But unfortunately, due to them hiding the secret and, in turn, protecting my abuser for all these years, we have not had the relationship we should have had, which is heartbreaking to me and more collateral damage from my abuse. Once again, due to no fault of my own.

What could my supposed protector have done better?

- For starters, they could have told my dad when they found out what was going on when I was a little girl.
- They could have asked me instead of assuming that the abuse had stopped.

- They could have taken me to the psychologist as a child more than once and not had my abuser sitting outside in the waiting room.
- Once they were aware of the abuse, they should have WATCHED AND LISTENED CLOSELY TO WHAT WAS GOING ON IN THEIR OWN HOME!
- They should not have made me sleep in the same room or bed as this person on holidays!
- They could have stopped letting my abuser get away with so much throughout their life.
- They could have asked me as an adult if I was ok.
- They could have asked what they could do to help me deal with my trauma later in life.
- They could have held my abuser to account, just once for what they did to me.
- **They most definitely should not have asked me to hug my abuser at my dad's funeral**! How could they think this was okay to ask of me, knowing what they knew, whether it was my dad's final wish or not?
- They could have validated my feelings just once! Instead of always putting my abuser's secret before my pain. (Circling the wrong person again).

People's dying wishes are important, but these people didn't live through my abuse. So how could they think what they want or feel they need is more important than my healing? Hugging my abuser wasn't going to make things right or ok. That ship had already sailed and putting that kind of pressure on me just made my dad's funeral so much harder for me to deal with. I nearly couldn't attend his funeral due to my anxiety and hurt from that request alone. On what was already such a sad and difficult day.

I don't feel good about saying these things about my family members. It hurts to put this down on paper. There are no winners here. **But when you put a band-aid on a gash, you can't expect it to heal!** But how long do we let these people give us their excuses?

I struggled daily with how writing this book may be taken by my supposed protector as I love them very much. But at the end of the day, this could help so many more people, and that's going to have to take precedence.

And that's why intra-familial sexual abuse, which is not dealt with, is so damaging and why this book needed to be written.

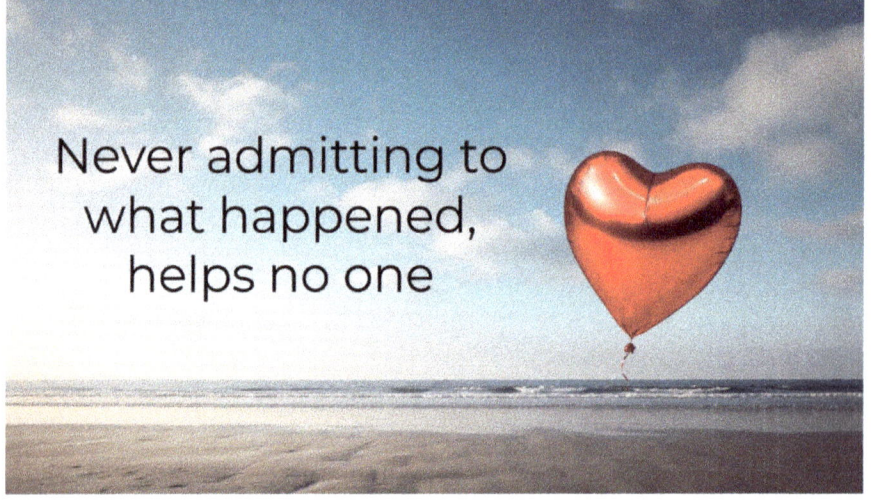

Chapter 12

The ongoing hurt

Part A

Personal ongoing hurt

Some people may think that child abuse victims need to move on and just get over it.

What these people don't understand if they haven't experienced childhood sexual abuse for themselves is that the hurt just keeps coming, and not just from the memories of the abuse.

It also comes in distress, rejection and abandonment from outside relationships later in life.

The family members who don't believe you or turn against you. The relationships you have lost due to telling your truth. Guilt-driven self-harm. Hurting yourself again and again to save others the pain. For example - staying around toxic people rather than causing a fuss by pulling away or bearing your trauma again and again, to keep the peace in your family and basically, putting up instead of standing up.

Example - The partner of your abuser who is now torn between your friendship and their spouse. So, they choose their spouse and bury their head in the sand about what their spouse did to you when you were a child. No doubt your abuser told them you are lying, or at best, a very watered-down version of events. So once again, you lose due to nothing you have done wrong.

I made my husband keep "the secret" for years. I used to think of it as my secret. But no longer am I that manipulated person. My husband knew what my abuser had done to me, but I still wasn't ready to let "the secret" out to everyone. Therefore, he had to be around the person who did this and that was very hard for him to stomach.

Is there any bigger decision in life to make than that of leaving and never seeing your family again? Breaking up with a significant other is a hard enough choice to make. But to pull away from your original family members is extremely difficult. The "choice" as I put it, is one that was made for us a long time ago. If not for being abused by a family member as a child, we would not be in this untenable position.

No wonder people's lives spiral out of control. How can you get your head around the fact that you keep losing in life due to no fault of your own? Why aren't people listening or caring? It comes back to moral worth. These people who keep letting you down are not from your circle of wagons. You need to find your people, and they are out there. You just have to move away from the "blindfolded bystanders" in your life and find "your people".

Blood may be thicker than water, but blood can turn septic, too.

The annual Christmas gathering

How do you deal with the family gathering you are expected to attend if your abuser, Uncle Bob, is there? The pressure you feel from your family to attend each year is overwhelming and abhorrent. Then the strain on you when mum tells you to go hug your Uncle Bob! That moment when your whole body just freezes at his touch, and your chest tightens as you temporarily stop breathing.

Your family won't ever understand how hard this is to deal with. The reason some people find this time of year so hard is because of these family get-togethers when your trauma is upgraded to extreme. What you may have been able to push down during the year is totally escalated. This can start even a month or more before the event with the decision you have to make about whether to go. The pressure you may feel from family to go versus the pressure you feel in your chest to not attend. So that four hours or more on just one day a year can be so detrimental to a survivor's health for weeks before and after the event. Mentally, physically and emotionally. Our eating, either the lack of or emotionally binge eating, can come into play. Sleep disturbance. Irritability affecting our relationships at home and work. So, our family members who push us to attend will have no idea how much damage this one day a year can do to us, just to keep them happy and keep the "family image" intact.

While I was still seeing my abuser in family settings, I was sick, anxious, and angry, a whole heap of emotions. This was before I had even gotten to the family gathering. I would often try to get out of family things, if possible. But the usual Christmas or birthday gatherings were inevitable. I found my perpetrator also didn't turn up quite regularly later in life. They often used excuses like they had things to do around the house. So, they felt awkward or guilty, maybe. One could only hope!

For me personally, I have felt a loss of the role of the person I grew up with and how they should have been my protector instead of the person who hurt me. They should have been my friend and one of the closest people in my life.

The ongoing hurt

I recently travelled overseas with a friend, and part of the trip was for her to visit with her sibling, who she loves. They have such a tight bond with each other, and it just reinforced what I missed out on. This makes me feel very sad that this was not my experience growing up or throughout my adult life. The tears that flowed from both of them when my friend was saying goodbye were heart-wrenching. I cried, too, but my tears were not only for them but also for what I never got to have and continue to miss out on.

My dad passed away about five months after I finally confided in him about what happened to me as a child. He was in his 70s by then. Part of the reason I didn't tell my dad earlier is because I was still protecting his relationship with my abuser. I knew once I had told my dad what this person did to me, it would hurt him also. I never wanted to hurt my dad. I also knew he would feel like he let me down, but he didn't because he didn't know.

My dad had a melanoma, and the cancer spread to his lungs and brain. I ran into my abuser at Palliative Care the day my dad died. I didn't know it then, but it would be the last day I would spend with my dad, EVER. My abuser disrespected me once again, as I should have expected after outing them for what they did to me. But I still tried to show them empathy regarding my dad and called their name three times. But they wouldn't turn around to face me, and all I got in response was "Got nothing to say to you." The emotions and anger, rage really, this stirred up in me were completely overwhelming. **So much anger and so much sadness in the one day.**

Anger at myself for allowing them to disrespect me again. Anger at myself for having empathy for someone who didn't deserve it. Anger at myself for letting them work me up when I should have been focusing my thoughts on my dad. Anger at my supposed protector for saying. "What did you expect?" when I went into my dad's hospital room and told them what had just happened. But mostly sadness that the last few minutes spent with my dad were filled with anger, arguments and raised voices and hoping he didn't hear or was distressed when he took his last breath.

I've never in my life experienced such primal raw emotions when I got the call half an hour later that he was gone. To have lost someone under these kinds of circumstances was excruciating.

I had driven away from the palliative care unit by then and had to pull into a fast food resturant's car park to turn around to go back. I still remember people in the restaurant staring at me and wondering what was happening as they could clearly see my distress, as I was sobbing so hard. I miss my dad so much, but I know he would be so proud of me for trying to help others get through their own pain and sadness.

Part B

Generational ongoing hurt

Consequences from child abuse can, in some situations, travel down through the generations in ways other than sexual abuse due to the ongoing abuse cycles that continue. It may start with the mum or dad who was sexually abused as a child. Then continue through to their children because the parents did not receive the help they needed to heal. These abusive, addictive or low self-esteem pathways then travel down through to their kids. Parents who don't go through the normal/proper milestones during their childhood due to their own abuse, do not develop fully as children. Therefore, there may be issues with their parenting as well into adulthood. This leaves them without the tools in life to parent as well as other non-abused people unless they end up receiving help.

Below are some aspects of an abused person's life that can be affected through the generations. Sometimes modelled by the child sexual abuse victim or their children or children's children. When no help is received along the lines of their family tree.

Education, decision-making, relationships, employment, accommodation and health.

Education

>Learning difficulties, difficult/disruptive temperament, low self-esteem, lack of confidence, giving up easily and doesn't try to learn, thinking they are dumb, anger issues, bullying of or from other kids, physical fights, loner, ostracised.

>All of the above can result in extra resources utilised like –

>Teachers' aids, time spent with heads of departments/principals, after-school extra help, or discipline like detention. Eventually, the child may leave school early and not get their full education. Which also leads to a further lack of confidence and poor choices in their lives.

Decision making

>No self-control, easily lead and manipulated, self-doubt, being used, people pleaser, abusive, temperamental, reckless, dishonest, untrustworthy, disrespectful.

>This may lead to substance abuse, being taken advantage of, no respect for authority, crime and eventually jail time.

And with women, there may be teen pregnancy, abusive partners, etc...

Relationships

Poor choices in friends/associates, abusive spouses, teenage parents, child support not paid/received, lack of care for own children, criminal gangs, mixes with bad crowds.

This can lead to further abuse of their children due to the kind of people they have around them. So, the abuse cycle continues onto another generation. They will no doubt not have a good relationship with their parents and siblings and be seen as the black sheep of the family.

Employment

Low-income due to lack of education, can't keep a job due to substance abuse/anger/unreliability, lack of opportunities in employment due to early school leaver and trouble with learning.

This can lead to always having a low income, potentially a lot of years on the dole, giving up on a career and not being a good role model for their kids.

Accommodation

Lives in low economic areas where crime/drugs and sexual abuse can be rampant, couch surfing, shared houses, bad elements living nearby, Refuges homelessness or jail.

Health

Lack of education regarding nutrition, low-cost - fast food, alcohol, smoking, drugs, bad oral hygiene, overweight or undernourished.

All these health issues can result from lack of education/poor choices growing up and can lead to health issues later in life, such as diabetes, liver or kidney damage, underweight babies, mental health diagnosis, heart disease, cancer and more.

So, one person's decision to molest a child causes such widespread and long-term damage not only to the victim but to so many generations that come after them. Not only harm to the individuals, but also, the amount of money that has to be injected into all the extra resources needed for the lifetime of an abused or generational abused person must be astronomical.

I have no idea how much money I have spent alone on psychologists, doctors' appointments, medications etc. throughout my life. Just to name a few resources expended.

Generational mistakes look away, look away.

Trapped in a snowglobe with nothing to say

Chapter 13

Stand by me

I have recently been trying to help someone close to me deal with their childhood sexual abuse from a family member. They have struggled with their trauma, mental health issues, substance abuse, trust issues and more. There has been a lot of toxicity in their extended family from the fallout of this abuse also. Unfortunately, due to their overwhelming trauma bond, I was unsuccessful in getting them away from their abuser and bystander. But I tried as hard and for as long as I could until it affected my mental health, too.

The kind of things we can do to help child abuse survivors are the following:

Show unconditional love

Unconditional love is a thing an abuse survivor may never have had. What they thought was love was the complete opposite. It was a toxic person taking self-gratification from them. Taking their innocence, their childhood and changing their lives forever. Taking away from them the person they should have been. How many words of love and healing this person needs, is endless.

Seek help

Most people won't have the faintest idea how to help someone struggling with child abuse trauma. It is so multifaceted and complex, who would know where to start? There are lots of organisations out there that can put you on the right track to help your friend or loved one. The internet is the best place to start, and you will find resources to guide you. Hopefully by now, they will have their own doctor or psychologist. But if they don't, they need to confide in one of these to get started. These professionals will also be able to recommend resources.

Comfort them

For goodness' sake, comfort them. They need this so badly. Tell them you are so sorry for what they have been through. They may have never had someone say that to them, and it will be such a relief to finally hear these words. Let them know there are people out there who do care. Make sure you show them empathy rather than pity, as pity may make them feel like you look down on them.

Build them up

Encourage them and tell them they are doing well. These simple words will help project them forward with their lives. Spend time with them—even outings such as going somewhere nice, like sitting in a park and relaxing for a while. Let them talk, really listen without interrupting or giving advice. Small things can lead to bigger goals in the future.

Educate them

Books explaining how abuse and trauma play out in people's lives. Programs such as Dr Phil, online blogs, etc... Anything to help them understand why they feel the way they do. Go to the library with them and find these books. Being able to understand why they feel this way is such a big part of healing. Tell them none of this was their fault, and let them know things will get better.

Set clear boundaries

Abuse survivors sometimes have problems with boundaries because of what happened to them. This is a very important point because you must protect yourself and your family if you are trying to help them. If there has been mental illness, substance abuse or violence in their life for example. You can't bring that into your home or amongst your family. You must let them know from the very start that if you are going to help them, there will be clear boundaries on what that looks like. You mustn't cave or they could take advantage of your kindness and generosity by pushing these boundaries. That helps no one in the end. They will lose a friend and you won't be able to continue to assist them.

Don't give up

I know I just said you have to set boundaries, or you won't be able to help them and don't give up sounds like a contradiction. But there are ways to continue to help someone even if that means passing the baton. You may need to help them in other ways, from a distance or by reaching out to other organisations. Even just sending positive messages to them regularly is still helping them. How are you going – you've got this – I'm proud of you – etc.. I'm hoping the person close to me mentioned above may read my book at some point, and this will help them finally move forward.

Help them, help themselves

By taking the seven steps above, you are helping them, help themselves. Like the line in the Tom Cruise movie – Jerry Maguire – "Help me, help you."

One day, they will realise they can do "life" by themselves and do it well.

They just needed some help and a few "Ata boys/girls" along the way from someone who cared enough to stand up for them. Sometimes, that's all that it takes. Like a kid being bullied in the schoolyard. When a friend stands up for them, they get an extra strength they may not have had alone.

Chapter 14

Fire collects all that it breathes

The sun has been ripped out of your sky,
The moon has been eclipsed,
And the stars have turned their back on you,
What is left but black?

I wrote this Poem to explain how abuse works in families who can't deal with the fallout.

This is how whole families turn against the victim.

The sun was their dad – their abuser, who should have been their hero.

The moon was their mum - their supposed protector, who should have been their saviour.

And the stars were their siblings - who turned away, should have stood with them, not against them.

No wonder they were lost.

Fire collects all that it breathes, is a perfect way to explain intra-familial childhood sexual abuse.

It is like an inferno that keeps growing within a family and sucks everyone around into an insidious vortex. Where nothing is right anymore and certainly nothing is fair for the victim.

Bystanders – ask yourself these questions if you are in any way considering brushing childhood sexual abuse from a family member under the rug –

- Did the perpetrator arrange to be alone with their victim – e.g., manipulate the circumstances for the act to take place?
- Did the perpetrator commit this act in secret?
- Did the perpetrator deny or minimise what they did, at least at first?
- Did the perpetrator only display regret once you caught them or found out for sure?
- Did the perpetrator tell you not to press charges and that they won't do it again?

All of the above shows that the perpetrator knew exactly what they were doing was wrong.

They were not regretful until they were caught, and only because they were caught! You should not believe them, and you should take whatever steps necessary to remove the child from harm and stop the current abuse. **Get ongoing help for the victim and go to the authorities. So this doesn't happen to another child!**

In murder cases, you are called an "accessory to the crime" if you see it or know details about it and don't come forward. So, you too, can be charged with a crime just by knowing about it. In family child abuse, this should also be the case. It may well be in some circumstances. But you will pay one way or another, so if that's your only motivation, get them help!

Putting something in a box and locking it away doesn't mean it will stay there forever. Someone will come along and unlock that box at some stage, whether it's the perpetrator abusing another child. Or it is the victim coming along, speaking their truth, and unlocking it. That secret will not stay locked in there forever! So, the bystander shutting that lid and turning that key needs to be very aware that this is not the end of the story. **THAT BOX WILL BE BLOWN WIDE OPEN AT SOME POINT!** Your inaction may well be responsible for another innocent child being abused.

Strength vs Control

Matriarch meaning –

- a woman who is the head of a family or tribe.
- an older woman who is powerful within a family or organisation
- "a domineering matriarch"

In a lot of households, the Matriarchs are the ones who have substantial control over the children and grandchildren in the family. **But control does not equal strength!**

- Control meaning – the power to influence or direct people's behaviour or the course of events.
- Strength meaning – the degree of intensity of a feeling or belief. Also, the emotional or mental qualities necessary in dealing with difficult or distressing situations.

The older women in our families or our mothers, may feel they have control over their children. Some find it very difficult to loosen that control as their children grow older and into adults. What then happens if they feel they are losing control is that they become manipulative in their quest for control, particularly if they have a narcissistic personality.

Because they have guided their children for so long, there is an innate feeling of having to do what their mothers say. But even bullies can control people without any real inner strength which doesn't mean they are strong or have strength of character. In fact, in some of our situations, these matriarchs are not able to stand up to the men in the family. Or don't want to lose contact or their relationship with these men. Therefore, we, as the abused children/siblings etc., become the scapegoats.

- Scapegoat meaning – a person who is blamed for the wrongdoings, mistakes or faults of others.

How does a woman come to terms with the fact that her husband has cheated on her? Not only cheated on her but had sexual contact with her own daughter? The fact that the younger version of herself has captured her husband's eye! The betrayal and anger she must feel would be overwhelming. Where does she put these feelings? Just like in my example later on in Chapter 25 – No good deed goes unpunished. Because she can't make sense of what has happened, the woman (mother) may eventually put her anger on her daughter, rather than her husband. Or even block it out so she doesn't have to deal with the unhealable situation she finds herself in. Women or men often blame the person their partner has cheated with instead of their partner. I unfortunately know someone who was the child in this situation. It's not my story to share the exact details of, but I'm sure they are not the only ones who have had to live this story. Far from it. It's just another example of a Matriarch "controlling" a situation and falsifying the narrative to fit what they need it to.

Being a strong woman is all about doing the right and moral thing for a child. Taking them away from a harmful, toxic situation and continuing to get them help. Speaking up and not silencing their children. **This is what a truly strong woman does!**

Janie's Got A Gun – Aerosmith – song released 1989

This song was written about a daughter exacting revenge on her father, who had been molesting her.

Steven Tyler said the lyrics were inspired by a Time magazine cover story about gun violence in the United States and a Newsweek article about children being abused in affluent suburbs.

This song was written in 1989 and is one of the few Aerosmith songs to deal with a heavy social issue.

So, it's not like intra-familial child sexual abuse hasn't been written about in decades past. So why don't we hear much about it? It's because it's taboo. Yucky subject. Depressing. People don't want to deal with it if it hasn't happened to them. So, let's all just pretend it doesn't exist, and then maybe it will go away! As Dr Phil says – "How's that been working for you?"

Chapter 15
The invisible perpetrator and the million-dollar question

Like a trick from a magician's bag, the perpetrators just disappear! Where did they go?

How do all these perpetrators keep getting away with their abuse? It is because of the family environment that the abuse happens within.

After disclosing to my adult son what happened to me, he looked at me and said, "Why did you keep seeing your abuser in family settings for so long if that happened to you?" And that's the million-dollar question, isn't it?

Why do we keep their secret and stay around them for so long?

There are a lot of reasons, and in each family, there will be slightly different ones. But the underlying fact is that we love the rest of our family, and don't want to lose them. We will also have very low self-esteem because of our abuse, and that makes any big decisions almost impossible. Or we may be trauma-bonded to our abuser or bystander. So basically, we are very vulnerable because of what we went through.

I stayed around my family for 44 years. During these times, I put up with feeling like a shadow of myself and let people walk all over my true feelings and emotions.

I had no help from the person who was supposed to protect me in this regard. They continually made me feel like I should keep the secret of my abuse, no matter what. I was told not to let my abuser's spouse (one of my best friends at the time) know. Don't speak about it to a psychologist I had started seeing, who was a friend of a friend of my abuser's spouse. I mean, come on! Why did my supposed protector think I was seeing a psychologist in the first place? They knew it was for me to deal with and get help for what my abuser did to me!

I was made to feel once again that my feelings, trauma and pain were less important than keeping their "sick secret." How did my supposed protector think that would make me feel? It made me feel traumatised and abandoned all over again. It made me have great anger towards them for putting my abuser's well-being over mine once again.

It didn't matter how much my supposed protector had helped me in other ways during my life or told me they loved me. Because always putting my abuser first trumped anything else they had ever done. What bystanders/supposed protectors can't comprehend is that by defending and protecting the perpetrator, they are putting the victim last and rejecting them all over again. This is a feeling the victim has felt their whole life.

And I have seen this happen again and again to abuse victims that I know. I am not sure I know of any whose supposed protectors have done the right thing, at least not at first.

I have seen adult sons turned against their mothers by the person who abused their mother when she was a little girl. I've heard people say – "oh, but you looked happy enough in that family photo!" Always trying to deflect the truth and question the victim's integrity.

Perpetrators use money, rumours, and lies to turn people against the victim, so that they can discredit the claims of abuse coming from the victim when they are heaped against them.

Particularly when the victim/survivor has turned to risky behaviours and lifestyles. Such as substance abuse, sleeping around, stripping, toxic relationships, etc.. Which is in fact a trauma response.

This makes it very easy for the perpetrator to ruin the creditability of their victim. As they can say they are a criminal, druggy, slut, crazy! Crazy is the one they love to throw in!

The perpetrator will try to convince the other family members that you can't believe anything the survivor says and that they are making it all up.

'Why did the survivor not say anything before?'

'Why did the survivor live with me or stay around me for so long if I did this to them?'

All of the above makes it easy for the perpetrator to convince others that they didn't do what they are being accused of.

Sadly, it is easier to believe the perpetrator due to the close/complex family situation. Because the ramifications of believing the survivor are, most of the time, just too difficult to deal with. Also, a lot of family members won't be able to understand how child abuse affects people into their adulthood. As I've stated in Chapter 2 - Putting out fire with gasoline and Chapter 9 – The snow globe effect.

So..... here's the million-dollar answer. The victim stays so long and becomes this way because of their childhood sexual abuse! The perpetrators become invisible and seem to disappear due to the family hiding the secret.

As mentioned in Chapter 2, the abuse we were subjected to changed us or made us do things to numb our pain. Whether it was substance abuse, self-harm, being a workaholic, being overly sexualised from a young age or developing a mental illness, all these things have manifested from the trauma of our abuse, and the perpetrator is responsible for how we turned out. YET, YET, they claim these reasons are why we shouldn't be believed. **UNBELIEVABLE, I KNOW!**

She seems crazy – because you abused her.
He does drugs – because you abused him.
She's a stripper – because you abused her.
He's in jail – because you abused him..........

I really hope this picture is becoming clearer!

Chapter 16

Grooming - it's not for animals

I think by now, we have all heard of grooming.

Grooming is what perpetrators/paedophiles do to gradually make children feel comfortable in their presence. So, eventually, they can molest/abuse them.

What this can look like –

Normalising touch in private places like hands under the child's bottom when sitting on the perpetrator's lap. Arm across the child's front/breast area, so, when they touch their breast area, they are accustomed to it already. Sometimes these actions are done in plain sight of others without other people realising, so the child feels that they can't complain or make a fuss. They feel trapped or think this must be normal, as no one around them is stopping it. Adults walking around naked is another way to make the child normalised to being around them unclothed.

Getting the child to go swimming, so they are exposed more in their bathers or if they are quite young, getting them to run around with nothing on.

Volunteering to babysit or take them for outings to give their parents a break. Gives a perpetrator easy access to a vulnerable child.

Pulling an adolescent girl's top up and making them feel like this is a normal thing to have done to them. Taking away their sense of privacy and safety can become commonplace in an abused child's life. Another technique perpetrators will use, especially in intra-familial circumstances, is for the family member (usually an adult) to tell their child that they are teaching them something, so they will be ready for their first sexual experience.

There are so many ways predators will gradually groom their victims over time, so when they are ready, they take it to the next/worst level.

I have had this done to me by more than just my abuser, and below are examples of what kind of events took place.

When I moved interstate, my friend's adult family member was trying to groom me.

Unfortunately for him, I knew what he was doing, and I wouldn't have a bar of it, even though I was only about 14 years old at the time it took place.

These are the kinds of things he did –

- Took me to the public pool, where he perved on me.
- Went out of his way to be nice, tried to make me think he was cool, and bought ice-creams, lollies, etc..
- He told us we could watch the tv downstairs one day, and when we turned the tv on, there was "girl on girl" porn playing, as he had left the video recorder playing on purpose. He was watching us from outside a window. A very full-on and obvious form of grooming.
- If my friend and I were lying on the bed upstairs watching TV, he would come and jump on us and try to tickle us, but

his hands went where they should not go. Besides the fact that this was just weird for an adult male to do to two adolescent girls. A thing my father would never have done.
- He grabbed me by the feet one time when I was wearing a skirt and held me upside down so he could see my underwear.
- That same day, he had to drive me home and told me he would buy me an ice cream. I kept telling him I didn't want one. But he wouldn't leave the shop until I ate it. He knew I was angry at him, and he was trying to "control the situation" as he didn't want me saying anything to my parents. He was such a creep.

It's amazing how, even though we may not have found the strength we needed to stand up to our abuser, when we see it happening to others, especially people we love, we dig deep and find that extra lion's strength to try to stop or speak out about another's abuse. I have heard of a young girl being abused by her stepfather, and it wasn't until she noticed his intentions leaning towards her own sister, that she stood up to him and told their mother.

Someone who had been abused as a child cried and asked me, "How do they know who to pick?" "How did they know they could do this to you and me, Deb?" I told her that it's called grooming. They do it slowly and carefully until they can tell who they will be able to easily manipulate and silence. Also, in what circumstances they can have access to a child. A trusting family member who is the child's parent, or a single parent needing help. Overworked parents needing child minding or easy-going, unsuspecting people who haven't been subjected to abuse themselves. So, they don't realise these monsters are walking amongst us. These people who abused us have been very cunning and manipulative. They've tested the waters, so to speak.

Another form of grooming came from a friend's older brother when I was in primary school. I was about 9 or 10 years old at the time. They had moved recently from overseas, and my friend insisted on me going to see the moving boxes in their garage area. I couldn't understand what the big deal was. But eventually, I went to see them.

My friend's 15-year-old brother was in the garage area waiting for me. It felt awkward, and he told me to show him my finger, which he proceeded to put in his mouth. He then tried to put his finger in my mouth. But I pulled away and wouldn't let him.

He was obviously wanting me to eventually put something else in my mouth, which I had no clue about back then.

I left that room as soon as I could and didn't return to her place again. I had that sinking feeling in my gut at the time. The feeling that tells you something is not right.

I had heard later of another girl at my school to whom he did the same thing.

I now wonder if the brother was molesting his sister, and she was trying to get other girls to take her place. I can't understand why a young girl would set her friends up like this otherwise.

I have also witnessed a family member pull his two adolescent daughter's shirts up in front of me and say – "how are your boobs coming in?" I was only a child when this happened, but it was so upsetting and confusing for me to think that this is how a dad would act. It made me scared at the time to think that this might happen to me also, by my dad. It didn't because my dad wasn't a weirdo.

I now think this person purposely did it in front of me for two reasons.

1. So, his daughters would feel this was normal because he did it in front of someone else. Or maybe his warped mind didn't realise it wasn't appropriate?
2. So, he could maybe turn his attention to me at some point.

The day my dad died, this same family member (not my abuser), came into the palliative care room, where we were all sitting while we were grieving. **I knew what this person was (a paedophile)**, but I couldn't say anything because of the circumstances. He sat next to me and put his arm around me. **I instantly went cold.** The immense rage feelings in me were almost uncontrollable. One of my family members (a younger female like myself), who knew what he was, saw my discomfort and casually took me away from him. **Just when I really needed my dad, he wasn't there.**

When I think about this situation and other times of discomfort when I had to be around abusers and not say anything, it is just amazing to me what I have had to deal with. Why should anyone have to be put through this kind of torment? Especially when they have just lost a most loved family member? Why? **It's because the older women in my family didn't speak up! Then, the younger females, including myself, have had to carry this terrible burden.**

Don't cry, little girl

Our worlds are so different,
But our lives have been the same,
Their words were so ignorant,
And we both have felt the shame.

Little girl, please don't cry,
The days will get brighter,
Only they believe their lies,
You'll always be my little fighter.

What I would tell you if I could go back,
You are beautiful, caring and smart,
Don't let them paint your future black,
The difference between you, worlds apart.

He was a small, darkened spirit,
Who could never match your light,
You saw it, you felt it, you feared it,
He was filled with ugliness and spite.

The war was waged against you,
The help just never came,
But you've always been filled with virtue,
And you would not play their game.

So, stand tall my little angel,
Look them right between the eyes,
No longer let them make you shameful,
You're so much stronger than their lies.

This woman has so much more to do,
So much more life in her yet,
We could only stop them once we knew,
And now they will repay their debt.

> This woman has so much more to do, so much more life in her yet

Chapter 17
The Confusion Within

"Angel and Devil" on your shoulders

Like in the cartoons we watched as kids, we all have an angel on one shoulder and a devil on the other. These confusing conversational "thought bubbles" that go back and forth over our heads.

Because of our low self-esteem and, at times our self-doubt, it is no surprise we all struggle with this. We had been mistreated, misguided, controlled, and confused for such a long time when we were little due to our abuse. So, this is now built into us, and it is very easy to find things to fight back and forth over in our own minds. Like a goat track you see on a hillside worn into the grass. My brain would have a rutted track between trying to make sense of what happened to me and forgiving the people involved. To standing up for myself and know just how detrimental the abuse was that I was subjected to. I am sure a lot of family child abuse survivors have this same goat track in their head. It is mentally exhausting trying to make sense out of it. Because, unfortunately, there is no good or right answer for us. As either way we turn, we lose. We either lose our family or we lose ourselves. And there is a great fear of no return also. The question is whether we will be believed and once we open our mouths to speak, there is no turning back.

Being extra sensitive can be quite normal for survivors, as some of us may have become overly responsive to stimuli and events in the world surrounding us when we were children. As I mention later in Chapter 27, Eyes wide shut, one of the signs of trauma in children can include obsessions with death or safety. This is what I encapsulated with my supposed protector as a little girl. Always needing to be around them and know that they were safe at all times. Another sign of childhood trauma is avoidance of school. I also talk about my experiences of this in Chapter 27.

I recently read an article about a study by Dr Charles Nemeroff from Emory University in Atlanta, USA – research released 2000.

At the university, they did a study of women who had been abused and others who hadn't.

They were all subjected to a simulated "social stress test." During this test, the women performed maths problems and did a mock job interview in front of an audience while having their heart rates and their levels of stress hormones monitored. The women who were abused, whether they were currently depressed or not, had elevated stress hormones. The doctor stated in this study – "Our interpretation is that early life abuse, sensitises a stress system. Once a new stress situation occurs, those individuals are more sensitised to the effects of the situation."

All of us have a certain vulnerability to stress that, once exceeded, can manifest itself in illness, such as depression or anxiety. But for these women, researchers say, the threshold of how much stress they can tolerate has been lowered. The abuse has rewired their stress hormonal systems to be either hyperactive or oversensitive.

But what the doctor also stresses in his findings is that people who have been abused should not feel hopeless due to these results. Current medications and psychotherapy can address these biological changes.

I think this kind of information is important to know. So, we, as adult survivors can better understand our overreactions or heightened sensitivities. And to find ways to help ourselves deal with stressful situations via – meditation, exercise etc., as I discuss in Chapter 29 Kaleidoscope.

I also feel that our friends and family members should be aware of our behaviours and actions. So, they can understand they are not that of someone who is just overly emotional or overreacting "per se" for no reason. But to realise why we tend to be this way.

Because we may sometimes, jump to the worst conclusion when we are adults, about people or how we think they are acting towards us, even if they don't mean us any harm. Then once we find out the circumstances were quite innocent, we will beat ourselves up about our overreaction. It is a vicious cycle, but one that is not uncommon to abuse survivors.

Our invisible anchors

You can't see them, but survivors of childhood sexual abuse, have these invisible anchors weighing them down, throughout their lives. Our anchor was originally attached to us, by our abuser. But after our abuse had stopped, and as we aged, we continued to carry these anchors, instead of handing them back to our abuser, where they belong.

So, the original anchor is our fear, pain and trauma from our abuse. The trauma of what we lived through as children. Then the anchor becomes the negative and toxic behaviours we developed as adults, due to our abuse.

The substance abuse anchor. The addiction anchor. The people pleasing anchor. The eating disorder anchor. The rage anchor. The mental illness anchor. The over-working anchor. The over-sexualised anchor. And the negative and toxic anchor list, goes on and on.

The anchor of confusion about what happened. What part we played in our abuse. Why we couldn't get out of the situation we were in, as children. The distorted questioning of "did we participate?" Why couldn't we stop what was happening? The "how I wish I could go back and do things differently" thoughts. Beating ourselves up mentally about what was never our fault, or doing in the first place. THE PERSISTENT ANCHOR OF DOUBT.

We inadvertently continue to hurt ourselves to try to navigate through what we can't understand. Treading water, whilst being dragged down continually by these anchors. It's just exhausting.

Our constant need for validation

Why do we seek approval from others? Our adverse childhood experiences and low self-esteem may influence why we seek approval or validation from others instead of ourselves. Having a fragile sense of worth makes it hard to validate our own experiences. We've lost confidence over the years to decide if what we are doing or feeling is right or wrong. This leads us to seek approval from others, to know if our thinking or feeling is justified. But if we put our faith in the hands of the wrong people, this can be devasting for our future.

It takes one to know one!

This is a saying we used as kids to retaliate when another kid called us a name in the schoolyard! Say if someone called you an idiot, you'd say – "takes one to know one!"

When you get to a better place from having dealt with your trauma, as I have, you may find you recognise traits in others that may be from their own childhood abuse trauma.

I'd rather sit with a real person any day, hold their hand while they open up, than be around a person who pretends they have it all together. That stiff upper lip rubbish. The ones who hold it together for the sake of appearances. I want to know about people's stories. These people are raw and real. I can understand other people who have experienced darkness. That's probably why I enjoy Stephen King's books so much, with his ability to create fully realised and relatable characters.

Some of my external anxiety responses later in life have been shaking or a shaky voice. Talking fast, overexplaining and overreacting to situations in which I felt vulnerable in. In my 20s and 30s, I used to scratch my hands, especially at night when the negative thoughts were the worst until they bled. I suppose this is similar to people who cut themselves to relieve their internal struggles.

My internal anxiety responses are that I can't sleep or stop thinking about a situation until it is resolved. My heart beating fast, and getting stomach cramps triggered by my IBS, to name a few.

So, if you see someone overreacting to a certain situation, maybe ask them if they are okay, rather than judging them on their response or overreaction.

Chapter 18
Who am I......really?

Being abused is like a death in some ways, you lose yourself.

Trauma changes us. We are not who we were born to be.

We are no longer as carefree as we started out in life. The blank slate has been written on, and the narrative was poor.

A child's formative years are between 0-8 years. This is the period when brain development is the fastest and what happens during this time can affect a child's mental and physical development and successes later in life.

When you hear me talk about a child's innocence in earlier chapters, I am talking about the normal stages a child should go through in a healthy environment, such as being carefree and able to learn and grow in a happy and protected space. **Feeling safe in their family home and have loving, caring people surrounding them.** The ability to just be a kid and have a wild imagination. To believe in Unicorns, Dragons, Santa, the Tooth Fairy, the Easter Bunny, etc.. To think that their mum or dad let the sun out in the morning and hang the moon and stars at night.

No child should ever have to think or worry about adult things like sex. That should happen a lot later in life when a person has had the milestones to develop enough to endure this new chapter. And it should not be bad and damaging to them because they are at an age where sex is a natural part and process of their life.

People ask – "why must you dwell on your abuse?"

They might as well ask why your eyes are brown. It's a part of you now and is not something that you can easily change.

My dad told me to – "move on Luv and just forget it." He didn't understand how upsetting and hurtful those words were to me at the time. To an abuse survivor, it says. It wasn't that significant. Just get over it.

But it was significant, and you don't just get over it.

My dad didn't know any better. He only knew what happened just before he got terminally ill, and of course, he wanted to keep his family together before he died. That is a natural response. But not something I could give him, unfortunately. I had already given too much of myself for too many years and wasn't willing or able to give anymore. I didn't have long with him before he died to tell him all I needed to say. As my focus changed from what happened to me to spending as much quality time with him and not burdening him any longer with my childhood abuse.

Every time someone uneducated or ignorant of what you went through says or does the wrong thing, you can question and lose a little bit more of yourself. **This is why you need to educate yourself about what happened to you.** Only then will you become knowledgeable and strong enough to not take on what people who have no idea what you've been through say to you.

I have personally learnt a lot from reading books and watching some episodes of Dr Phil or other similar programs about abuse and trauma. As well as learning from the world around me and the people I've spoken to about their own battles.

Some people may shy away from reading about or watching programs similar to what happened to them. But for me, it was about learning why I felt the way I did and relating to others who have been through similar circumstances. This is a very important message. I will explain why later.

I've also witnessed grown adults (real tough people) break down when talking about their childhood abuse.

They are taken right back to that moment when they were vulnerable and scared little kids, and it is just heartbreaking to see. It is such a raw and guttural pain that you can see they are reliving.

If we don't acknowledge our past and what happened to us, we can't move on to a better future. Similar to people trying to delete bad and ugly history. We need to learn from the wrongs that were done so we don't repeat them.

Someone asked me why sexual abuse victims are called "Survivors" later in life. But what other name is there, though? We are not or should not see ourselves as victims anymore because we need to move forward from what happened to us. What happened will always be in our past. But we need to see ourselves as people who have lived through and overcome. So hence the word - Survivor.

Or maybe, as my good friend said to me recently – you will go from –

Victim to Survivor to Victor

Once you've taken your power back and found yourself.

So, what does it mean to take your power back? This message I talk about all the time.

Well, for me, it means that I have become a confident person from learning as much as I could about childhood sexual abuse. I am a person who no longer allows others to dominate my emotions, reactions or feelings or to make me overthink what is important to me. If a situation escalates, I use my breathing to calm myself. I don't speak reactively, but calmly, to get my message across and my thinking has become so much clearer since pulling away from controlling people. I make sure I'm not drawn into any toxic discussions or negative narratives; someone is trying to pull me into. I will say no to things that I no longer want to do. Instead of just keeping others happy so they will like me, as I have done as a people pleaser in the past. I have found things I like to do in my life and will make time during the week to do these things, instead of overburdening myself with other people's wants or needs. Or to let anyone make me feel guilty for saying no. I will distance myself from or cut people out of my life who are not healthy for me. Even family members or people I once considered to be close friends. I will support and help people until...... Until they show me disrespect or that I am not important to them. Or they are still not helping themselves get out of toxic situations.

You can't continue to live in the victim role if you want your life to get better. You must drag yourself out of that rabbit hole. **Fill that dirt in, jump on it and compact the shit out of it.** So you can't go back. That's what I mean about taking your power back.

Change

There is a great line in the movie – "Life as a House" – released 2001.

George, who is played by Kevin Kline is one of my favourite actors. He says this line to his son struggling with his own life, and I have always remembered it.

You know the great thing, though, is that change can be so constant you don't even feel the difference until there is one. It can be so slow that you don't even notice that your life is better or worse until it is. Or it can just blow you away, make you something different in an instant.

I'll let you take from that what you will. But it left a great impression on me.

Every person and every personality is different. As every circumstance of abuse is different, and everybody's reaction to abuse is different. At every age, you will handle your trauma in a different way from how you handled it at an earlier age. Or at a later age. But no one should ever beat themselves up or worry that they could have dealt with things differently. Because you did the best with what you had and knew at the time.

BUT ONCE YOU KNOW BETTER, YOU MUST DO BETTER!

Father, I fell

Dad, I found a card today,
That you'd written me on my birthday,
It was usually Mum's job to write,
And there'll be no more now, you've gone away.

As a little girl, I clung to mum,
Didn't give you a chance, now I feel so numb,
Wish I could turn back time, and give you a hug,
All those years you were there; I took for granted.

Playing on the beach, you showed me a shell,
Put it to my ear so I could hear the waves,
Never knowing your little girl was going through hell,
Oh, how I wish I could bring back those days.

You taught me tennis, I got really good,
But along to their matches, I'd always be dragged,
I wish now I'd told you, if only I could,
But they were the star, so behind them, I lagged.

It wasn't in our nature, to push or be bold,
So much like my dad, I just never knew,
But you with a racquet, were a force to behold,
I hoped one day, you'd be proud of me too.

Mum stayed silent, didn't want to burden you,
The night she caught them, you were fast asleep,
Tired with your own worries, as all good dads do,
So, there in the dark, alone did she weep?

I know that you were worried about me,
Couldn't understand why, I did what I did,
But it wasn't my job, to make you see,
How could I tell you; I was just a kid.

I know you're still here, and you're proud of me now,
Giving me the courage, to write about my youth,
To help other survivors, move forward somehow,
Oh, father I fell, but now here's my truth.

This is an Ode to my dad Lenny, who was such a kind and gentle man. I wish I had let him into my struggles a lot earlier in my life. Then maybe our time together would have been better.

Chapter 19

Everybody's childhood plays itself out

You cannot be an adult in this or any society until you've finished with your childhood –words from my favourite author - Stephen King.

You can't block out your childhood. Whatever you went through will make its way back to you at some point when you are an adult.

You can't run away from yourself! **YOU have to deal with YOU.**

It's not anyone else's job to do, either. It's up to you, and that may not seem fair. But you are the only one who can do the hard work to get you to a better, healthier, and more stable place in your life.

If you are not willing to learn, nobody can help you,

BUT IF YOU ARE WILLING TO LEARN, NOBODY CAN STOP YOU!

Relationships are not singular though; the people you choose to have in your life will need to help and support you. If they don't, they are not your people. Distance yourself from them, as they will only keep you down.

But if you are brave, it will all come out in the wash, as they say, and the ones who doubted you will start to respect you more.

Once you tell your truth and be proactive, not reactive, things around you will change. You will find a new strength in yourself that you wouldn't have felt before you started telling your truth and standing up for yourself.

And it is not your job to convince others that you are telling the truth!

Just stand true to yourself, and maybe they will come around to seeing that you are not doing this to them. But for you!

Surrendering to change is so important in your journey to healing. Stop fighting to keep your old ways and mentality. It was unhealthy and unhelpful to you. Let people in who want to help you and are good for you.

With family abuse, it will be a tough slog, as I have mentioned before, as no one wants to do the hard work to help a survivor. Not when close long-term relationships will be tested, ugly facts dealt with, and hard decisions made. **But keep remembering you are doing this FOR YOU, not to them.**

And if somebody doesn't like the message I'm sending. There are three possible explanations –

1. They have abused a child, and they are scared that the victim (now survivor) will come after them and hold them accountable for what they did and don't want the survivor to receive my message of strength and healing.
2. They are a victim/survivor themselves and are not ready to admit what happened and tell their story.
3. They have been a bystander and are unwilling to finally admit and help their family member.

Whichever way, I see it as a step forward, as my message is getting through.

Chapter 20

Trauma-induced emotional immaturity vs Bystander emotional immaturity

Some people can be quite intelligent but sometimes seem very immature or overreactive.

And I am not talking about the clowning around type of immaturity. But they are emotionally immature and may seem very overreactive or extremely aggressive without much provocation.

So, there are two parts to this chapter.

1. Trauma-induced emotional immaturity.
2. Bystander emotional immaturity.

I'll begin with no. 1 – Trauma-induced emotional immaturity.

When you see someone highly sensitive or reactive to something that wouldn't normally bother you, you may be witnessing someone who has been traumatised and their reaction to some kind of stress response that is being triggered by their past abuse.

1st example – someone cuts them off in traffic, and you see a volatile reaction, and maybe even a road rage type situation occurs. This person is reacting to the unfairness of what they feel someone has just done to them. It is not really a big deal in the whole scheme of things for a non-traumatised person, but the traumatised person has a hair-trigger response that can be set off at any time because of their previous abuse. But we can't operate, fired up! All our control, both physical and verbal, just goes out the window when we try to operate in this highly stressed condition.

2nd example – someone is lying to them, and they know they are being lied to.

The traumatised person may take this very personally and hold it against that person for a long time. They will find it very hard to trust people; once that trust is broken, it is a huge deal.

3rd example – someone is taking advantage of them. This is a huge trigger for a traumatised person. This is what happened to them in their childhood. Obviously, it is a different scenario, but it may still have the same effect on them later in life. They will feel vulnerable, insecure and angry and also question why someone would do that to them again. Questioning why is a big part of their life. Why would someone want to hurt me? Why me? Why do I have to struggle because of what happened to me when I was young? These kinds of questions persist throughout their life.

When trauma impairs a young person's ability to develop it can freeze their emotional response at the age they experienced their trauma. This is known as arrested psychological development and is also similar to age regression. In short, they react emotionally at a much younger age than they actually are and can cease taking responsibility for their actions and lives. It's all about not feeling in control.

Some examples of this are –

- Addictions
- Immaturity
- Anger
- Fear
- Blame
- Resentment
- Confusion
- Greed
- Shame

2. Bystander emotional immaturity.

This is not the real name for what I am about to tell you. Just something I have observed.

Bystanders "can't handle the truth!" Like the line from the movie – "A Few Good Men."

Bystanders can't deal with what they have seen or now know happened to a victim. So, they shut their eyes, block their ears and stick their head in the sand. Especially the older generations, as this is how their parents taught them to deal with abuse in the family.

I have personally experienced this scenario when telling a relative about how a family member abused his own daughter.

There was a blankness on my relative's face. Then, denial about the abuse came from their mouth. Then they said, "I am hungry, I have a headache, do you want a sandwich?" They said. "Isn't she (the victim) just making it up because she's mentally ill?" Aha, the old crazy excuse! They also said. "But wasn't she just little when this happened?" I think some people have the misinterpretation that it isn't so bad if abuse happened to us when we were kids! Like it happened so long ago that you should have forgotten about it or gotten over it by now or something?

But it is especially bad because it happened when we were kids. And to try to justify someone abusing their daughter at any age is beyond belief.

I was gob-smacked that that was their response to hearing this disturbing news.

And to make things worse, they still see the person who abused his daughter and have never questioned him or held him accountable.

But should I be surprised? They are from the "brush it under the rug" generation.

This generation is the biggest problem for sexual abuse survivors. They were taught to keep it a secret. Keep it in the family. Oh, it was kept in the family, alright!

This kind of response disgusts me! There are no other words to explain how angry it makes me feel, and I no longer have any more tolerance for people who behave like this.

They seem to lack emotional intelligence, insight and maturity, and they don't want to educate themselves or do the hard work to help the survivor. So, they block it out or minimise the damage done to the child, now an adult.

Emotional intelligence is having the ability to –

- Be self-aware
- Self-regulate
- Internal motivation
- Have empathy
- Have social skills

I know if I gave my supposed protector this book, they would most likely refuse to read it. Because they don't want to know about "that stuff." If they knew the hard facts they might have had to face the truth. But they probably feel way too ashamed or guilty to do that. They couldn't live with themselves if they faced what happened and all the negative ways it has affected my life. And this is the sad part. Because they refuse even to try to understand, they will never have the relationship they should have with their family member - me. They are still circling the wrong person which will be their legacy to the survivor - me.

It needn't be this way at all if they had just once really tried to understand. I know they couldn't change what happened at the time before they knew. But what they didn't do after the fact is why I still struggle to this day.

The family connection to my abuser certainly didn't change the experience for me. It might have changed it for my bystander, as they wanted to ignore/dismiss it. But it made it even more distressing for me to have it be a family member who abused me rather than a stranger. Due to the constant contact I had to have with them and the feelings of disgust and shame I carried for so long.

Chapter 21

Generational abuse

Only an awakened mind can repel monsters – Stephen King

I've previously mentioned abuse that goes unpunished and hidden within families.

Because of this, the abuse seeps down to more generations and the toxicity and trauma continue.

Fact – In up to 90% of child sexual abuse cases, the offender is known to the family.

Like my example in Chapter 9 – The snow globe effect. The uncle abused his nephew due to the uncle previously being abused by his grandfather. Therefore, we may presume the nephew may go on to abuse a member of his own family, when he is older or a friend, etc., due to his own abuse, and this insidious cycle will continue again and again and again…….

Because it is like a disease that is passed on to the next person once they've been exposed to it. Particularly with men.

Insidious meaning – proceeding in a gradual, subtle way, but with very harmful effects.

In my experience, women seem to be the main party keeping these secrets hidden.

My supposed protector was a woman. My family member, who was abused, was let down by her mum, another woman. So many women become the supposed protectors/bystanders in these situations because the kids tell their mums what's happening, rather than their dads, because most kids feel closer to their mums when they are little.

It's a shame more kids aren't able to tell their dads what's happening. I wish my dad had been allowed to know when I was a kid. That opportunity was taken away from him. Even though he didn't have the strongest personality, I think he would have found that strength if he knew what was happening to his little girl. **This could have changed my whole life!**

Why do women keep these shocking secrets to themselves and not do anything about them? The awful truth is just like the Matriarchs I spoke about in Chapter 14, who use control to keep their family members quiet. These women can't handle what's happening.

But we should be banding together as women, not dividing.

Not all perpetrators are male. But all the ones I have had experience with or heard about personally have been. And their wives, sisters, mothers, grandmothers and aunts have all kept their secrets. Why?

We should protect our daughters, sons, siblings, grandchildren, nieces, nephews etc.

If only the people who knew spoke up and held the abusers to account when it first happened, they may stop the next generation or more of their own family members from being abused.

It is like letting a murderer off. Once they get a taste for it and there is no punishment **THEY WILL CONTINUE!** Why wouldn't they? They are sick individuals who are not being held to account and know they can get away with it.

Society doesn't want to acknowledge that a family member could hurt a child in this way because it's taboo to talk about. But we need to be a society where there are consequences for actions.

If you think something may have happened to your child, don't be judge and jury. Take them to a professional like a psychologist or doctor to determine and **LOOK FOR SIGNS!**

THIS NEEDS TO STOP NOW!

I have been told my whole life not to say anything. But I will do the exact opposite if it helps just one person to be spared the trauma that I and many others have experienced. And quite frankly, I am tired of picking up the pieces where previous generations have dropped the ball. People can say "Don't rock the boat" all they like, and some people may be able to look the other way. Not me.

Because every which way I look, it's there, staring me right in the face. I have no choice but to call this sick behaviour out. Or I wouldn't be able to look at myself in the mirror each day, and I have to do what my heart says I should.

I am the sum total of my family's generation of females, and I won't be taking the easy road like the previous generations have. Writing this book has been a watershed moment for me, and it hasn't been without pain and heartache. I've always had pain and heartache, but of a different kind. The kind of pain that being silenced gave me. The frustration of words unsaid and peace kept at the victim's expense. Which is no peace at all in the end. Even the perpetrators must feel anxiety of some kind, never knowing when or if they will be exposed. As for the bystanders, well, they must feel guilt for not speaking up and some kind of pain for what they have seen happen to their family member.

I feel a great responsibility to do this work and show the future females of my family and others **that it is not okay to be treated this way!** Or to be silent when they see something wrong. I also urge the males to speak up if they know something or have had something happen to them. **The power of a male telling a male that it's not ok - is Momentous!**

Nobody is immune from doing the right thing. This is everyone's job to fix, whether they want to or not and I'm hoping my book will finally shake some people awake!

My abuse has seeped down to my children in a different way, too. This is also what I mean by generational abuse. I became the mother who watched her children closely while they were growing up. I watched who their friends were. Who their friends' parents and particularly stepparents were. I watched who their friends' siblings were. And when they were asked for a sleepover, this was a very tough time for me emotionally. Just hoping they would be safe and know what to do if anything happened while I wasn't around. Unfortunately, I also watched their relationships with each other. No parent should ever have to do this. But because of what happened to me, it was something I had to make sure didn't happen with my own children. Luckily all my kids are well-adjusted and very caring individuals who would never go there. They all have healthy relationships with each other.

So, the question has been put to me. What would I do, as a mum, if I found out one of my children had been abusing their sibling?

And sure, that's a fair question, as I totally realise what a hard place this is to be in. I have empathy for the parents in this situation. So here are my answers –

- I would seek ongoing treatment from a psychologist for BOTH of my children.
- I would make sure there was never another opportunity for my child to be abused by their sibling again, in whatever form that needed to take.
- I would make the abuser admit what they did to the victim.
- I would make sure the abuser didn't have access to any other vulnerable children.
- I would ALWAYS make myself available to the victim/survivor whenever they needed me throughout their entire life.
- I would never discredit or belittle the feelings of the survivor.
- I would never silence or mute the survivor from telling their story or seeking punishment against the abuser if the circumstances permitted.
- If separate family gatherings were needed later in life by the survivor I would not hesitate to let them know that was ok.

No one's to blame?

Throughout writing this book, I thought of a title first and then wrote the content within it. Or the content came to me, and I searched for an appropriate chapter title or subtitle. This subtitle "No one's to blame?" I have purposely put a question mark after.

Generational abuse

This is because it depends on your perspective. The age-old debate of whether you can blame a perpetrator for abusing another child after they themselves have been abused as a child. I have my thoughts on this, which are fairly evident throughout this book. But others may have a different opinion.

What I am about to show you is a hypothetical illustration of generational intra-familial sexual abuse and I am using colours instead of people's names. Perhaps this example of a messed-up family tree will help you make a clearer decision on just who you think is to blame.

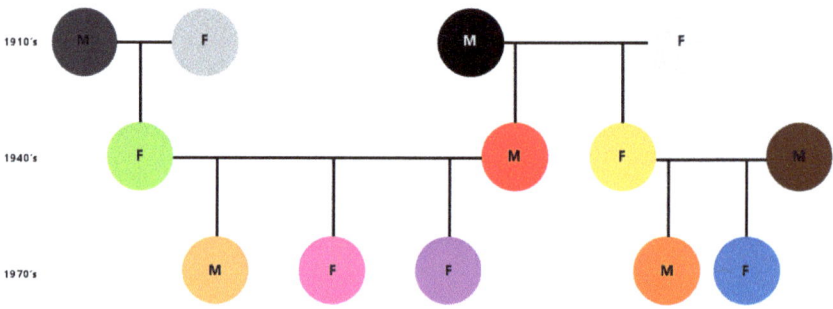

- (M) - indicates male (F) - indicates female
- The generation born in the 1910's – Grey (M), Silver (F), Black (M), and White (F)
- The generation born in the 1940's – Green (F), Red (M), Yellow (F). Brown (M) – newcomer, not of either family tree.
- The generation born in the 1970's – Gold (M), Pink (F), Purple (F), Orange (M) and Blue (F)

Family 1
Grey (M) marries Silver (F)
Offspring – Green (F)

Family 2
Black (M) marries White (F)
Offspring – Red (M) & Yellow (F)

Family 3 (next generation)

Family 1 offspring Green (F) marries Family 2 Offspring Red (M)
Offspring – Gold (M) Pink (F) Purple (F)

Family 4 (also next generation)

Family 2 offspring Yellow (F) marries newcomer Brown (M)
Offspring – Orange (M) Blue (F)

So, these family trees will show generational abuse travelling down through their branches.

(1910's parent – Grey) abuses his (1940's daughter – Green).

Green (teenager now) becomes highly sexualised and attracts the attention of Red (teenager now). Red is also highly sexualised as a young male, and he ends up marrying Green. Red and Green have (1 son - Gold) and (2 daughters - Pink and Purple).

Green over the years tires of Red's constant sexual needs. This leads Red to turn his attention to his and Green's daughters and he sexually abuses both Pink and Purple. But Red also abuses his nephew Orange when he is a young boy, the son of Red's sister Yellow. Orange, being sexualised, then goes on to abuse his sister Blue when she is a little girl.

1940's generation - Yellow was abused by her brother Red during their childhood. This may be what leads Red to think he can get away with abusing his own daughters, Pink & Purple, later in life.

Yellow told her mother, White, about her brother, Red, abusing her when she was young. Her mother silenced her and told her not to talk about it again.

Green told her mother, Silver, about her father, Grey, abusing her. But she was also told not to talk about it. Therefore, no help came for either Yellow or Green (both 1940's females).

Generational abuse

Ok, to recap. Grey 1910's, Red 1940's and Orange 1970's become the abusers in the family (all males).

Green 1940's was abused by her father. Yellow 1940's was abused by her brother.

These females were both silenced when seeking help from their mothers. Sadly, neither Green nor Yellow talks to each other about their abuse when they become sisters-in-law.

1970's kids of Yellow and Brown.

Orange has now been abused himself as a child. He is the son of Yellow and Brown and the older brother of Blue. Orange was abused by his uncle, Red, (Brother of Yellow).

Orange, due to being sexualised, goes on to abuse his little sister, Blue, when they are both young. Blue tells her mother, Yellow, about her brother, Orange, abusing her. But Yellow doesn't offer any help because her mother, White, didn't help her. So little Blue doesn't get any help, and the abuse continues.

1970's kids of Green and Red.

Purple and Pink are both abused by their father, Red. Pink doesn't tell anyone what happened to her. Purple tells her mother, Green, but Green offers no help because she received no help from her mother, Silver, when her father, Grey, abused her.

This is how the toxic patterns form in these intra-familial family circumstances.

So Green was abused by her father, Grey, and then her daughters, Pink and Purple, were abused by their father, Red. This exact same abuse has been duplicated to Green's daughters, who their mother has also muted.

Yellow was abused by her brother, Red, and then this same abuse was duplicated to her daughter, Blue, who was abused by her brother, Orange. Blue has also been muted by her mother, Yellow.

When we look at White being the grandmother of Blue, Pink and Purple, you can see that all three of her granddaughters were abused by the males in the family.

100% of her granddaughters! Not 1 out of 3, but 3 out of 3! These statistics are staggering!

White's own daughter, Yellow, doesn't help her daughter, Blue, due to the continuance of the silencing throughout the generations. This abuse was allowed to continue due to Red never being held to account or punished by his parents, Black and White, when he was a boy and abused his sister, Yellow.

Red (1940's) has caused Orange (1970's) to take up this same insidious behaviour. Passed on this heinous "disease" so to speak! So, Red has destroyed two families with his predatory behaviour. Not just his own family but his sister, Yellow's family, too.

If Green wasn't abused by her father, Grey, she might not have allowed her own daughters, Pink and Purple, to be abused, or at least acted appropriately, with help and not silence, when she found out.

You can see how this abuse can continue down through family trees due to the silence and non-accountability taken. Every generation of this family continues to have at least one perpetrator. 1910, 1940 and then 1970.

No one's to blame?

Yes, I suppose that's true. No one person is to blame! There are so many people to blame.

Generational abuse

The abusers are to blame. The "abusers" "abused victim" who carries it on to the next person/generation, are to blame. The bystanders who have silenced the victims/survivors are to blame. The survivors who then don't speak about their own abuse are to blame.

NO ONE PERSON IS TO BLAME! THAT'S EXACTLY RIGHT!

THEY ARE ALL TO BLAME FOR THE CONTINUED GENERATIONAL ABUSE AND SILENCE!

Chapter 22

Be a good CHAP

Don't let your children swim in the same waters that drowned you.

Childhood abuse prevention is everyone's business.

NOMW – not on my watch - is my motto.

Being a good chap means being a good **CHILD HOOD ABUSE PROTECTOR.**

If you know something, do something! Help the child abuse victim; don't turn away no matter how hard it may seem. No matter how close you are to the perpetrator or whatever family connection there may be.

You have a duty to protect the innocent and vulnerable, and it is just morally the right thing to do. You may be responsible for stopping generational abuse, which is huge. You may stop your grandchild from being abused and end the abuse cycle in your family.

Want to be a good bystander? There is no such thing! And I'm not talking about an innocent bystander.

Bystanders who know about child sexual abuse and do nothing are weak and just as bad as the perpetrators.

In fact, the bystander, in a lot of cases, is the person the survivor dislikes the most, later in their lives. They will most likely still be in the survivor's life and will be a huge trigger for them. Even if the survivor doesn't see their perpetrator anymore, they will always be reminded of their trauma because the bystander did nothing. Well, it would be considered more than nothing. They kept a terrible secret or told their family member to keep it to themselves. And every time that bystander lets the survivor down again later in life, it will be a much bigger deal. Because the survivor is just waiting and expecting it. So, the survivor will most likely have an overreaction to the disappointment they feel once again. **The bystander may feel like they can never do anything right, and it's all due to what they did wrong when the survivor was a child.**

I have heard of a young man who was raped by his own brother. He finally got up the courage and told his mum, but she didn't believe him or get him help. He went on to have severe anger issues, hated women and struggled to keep jobs as his temper was so explosive. All because of his abuse and his mum not believing or helping him. So, he would have lost most of his family due to firstly being abused and then not being helped.

A lot of men struggle with their sexuality after being abused by a male when they were young. They may think they are gay or not be sure because a male abused them, and that adds an extra layer of confusion to their trauma. As humans, we are great at blaming ourselves for things we have no control over. This is a disheartening reality.

I want to try to reach as many men as possible with my book. They are the ones that history shows us will most likely not ask for help and potentially reoffend. Women have tended to be more empathic in years gone by. But there are a lot of men these days who show a great deal of empathy, too.

I don't want men struggling and blaming themselves for what happened to them as children, while still trying to be the strong men our society expects of them. Going to work every day and being eaten up inside by this silent enemy. By helping the abused men in our society, it will, in turn, help future children from being abused. That's a win-win, in my opinion.

Don't let your kids become a statistic because you aren't strong. This isn't going away; you can mark my words. Their anger, anguish and pain from their trauma will just grow more extreme and get worse if you don't act. You need to get them help when they are young, or you will be the one they take their fury out on when they are older.

And this is why we must speak out.

My next poem is for all the men out there who need to hear it xo

Hey Silence

You are always there, my darkened friend,
Even through the rush, rush, rush,
Out of nowhere, we hear your black descent,
Again and again, we await your crush.

As a child, we'd always catch our breath,
Our souls we'd try, to hide away,
But you'd yank us to, your pitch-black depths,
And down, down, down, you'd make us stay.

Like Pinocchio, Geppetto's puppet toy,
Strings pulled from places high above,
But it wasn't a toy, it was a real boy,
And what you've done, is far from love.

Hey silence, you took his words from him,
Though he tried so hard to get them out,
Came close at times, our poor boy Jim,
But kids have so much doubt, doubt, doubt.

Years went by, and you stayed in his head,
Blaring silence gave rise, to his inner violence,
The mind replays, what the heart can't forget,
But he waited and watched you, from a distance.

You're an old man now, on shaky legs,
Jim's just one of many, that silence took,
But the tree remembers, what the axe forgets,
And this boy's strength, you should not overlook.

See that young man, coming down the lane,
Does he look familiar, it's kind of hard to say,
You smile, but it quickly turns to pain,
Before you speak, silence takes YOUR words away!

There's others too, standing strong with Jim,
It's their turn now, watch them all arise,
Names you don't remember, it's just him, him, him,
Your old mate silence took your alibis.

Young men, please don't go the way of him,
That old man was weak, and he did you wrong,
Your souls are just waiting, in the wings,
Hey Silence, no more, they've become too strong.

Chapter 23
Trauma Bonding

Trauma bonding occurs when an abuser repeats a cycle of abuse with another person, in this case, a family member.

Because the victim also looks upon this person as their protector, the victim requires validation from their abuser. This would seem strange and hard to understand to most people who haven't been in this situation. But if the person is a family member that is abusing you, you may want so badly to keep your connection to your family member that you have this toxic relationship with them. Although they are causing you pain, you still rely on them for comfort. This generally happens in a child/parent relationship. Your trauma bond may also be between you and your supposed protector. Which may be your mum if your father or brother was abusing you, and she is the bystander/supposed protector.

Signs of trauma bonding –

- Agreeing with the person's reasons for treating you badly.
- Trying to cover for the abusive person.
- Argue with or distance yourself from people trying to help, such as friends or family members.
- Become defensive or hostile if someone tries to intervene or stop the abuse, even if it's a police officer who is trustworthy.

- Being reluctant to take steps to leave the situation.

Unhealthy attachments –

Humans form attachments as a means of survival, and babies become attached to their parents, whom they depend on. So, when someone's main source of support is also their abuser, a trauma bond can develop. So, as mentioned above, even though their caregiver has hurt them, they also look to this person for comfort when, they are hurt in other ways.

Dependence –

When a child relies on their parent for love and support, if that parent is abusive, the child may come to associate love with abuse and believe this association is normal. As this is all they have ever known.

The child may also come to blame themselves for this abuse as a way of making sense of what is happening to them. "He says he loves me so much; they are under a lot of stress; I don't want them to leave, so I put up with it, or it's all my fault, I know they are sorry," etc.

This allows the abuse to continue.......

Attachment and dependence with my supposed protector –

When I was about halfway through primary school, I started regressing emotionally back to a younger age. This came in the form of wanting to be around my supposed protector at all times. My understanding of this kind of regression period in my life has only just recently become clearer, as I've learned more about childhood abuse and trauma. If my supposed protector were late picking me up from school or any activities, I would panic. Worse-case scenarios entered my head. My usual thought was that they had died in a car accident, and that's why they weren't there to pick me up. Another time, I remember being dropped off at a night-time primary school disco.

The "flight" trauma response hit me out of nowhere. I was about to enter the disco when I just started running back to the car park. Where my "safe person" had just dropped me off. My "safe person" was how I saw my "supposed protector" as a child.

The door attendant tried to stop me, and I lied and said it was okay, my parent was still there. I managed to get to their car just as they were driving off and went home with them.

Another time we were on holiday at a relative's house in a different state, and the parents were all going out for dinner. The kids were to stay at home, probably with a grandparent or someone. I was distraught and tried everything I could to be allowed to come along. I was about twelve years old by this time, which should not have been a problem for someone my age.

Sleepovers at friends' houses also became impossible. I was too worried about potentially having that flight response kick in, and I didn't want my peers to think I was a baby. So, I avoided sleepovers from about 12 years old, even though I used to love them at a younger age. I still remember my best friend from high school thinking I must have wet the bed which was why I would never sleep over her house. This was very embarrassing for me to have kids think that way. If only she knew the real reason back then!

Speaking of my best friend from high school. She recently contacted me after she read an article about my childhood abuse. It was on a child sexual abuse protection organisation's website, (Bravehearts), in their survivor stories section. Once again, I didn't name my abuser in this article. She was my best friend in years seven & eight when I lived on the Northern Beaches of Sydney. In her message to me, she guessed who my abuser was. She told me she had seen my abuser grab me on my chest, as we walked past them, on multiple different times, when she came over to my house. She told me I yelled at my abuser often and was very angry and looked embarrassed whenever this occurred. **But my abuser just laughed!** My friend told me she couldn't understand at the time why my abuser was doing this to me. She said she used to think, what the hell are they doing?

This message hit me very hard for multiple reasons. Firstly, I had forgotten this part of my abuse. I had either blocked it out or it was a regular occurrence. So, it didn't stay in my memory. Then I realised just how old I was by that age! Thirteen or fourteen when I knew this friend, and my abuse was still continuing. Also, the fact that this was allowed to continue after I had confided about my abuse to my supposed protector. So, my abuser knew they could get away with it, as they weren't punished or held to account. Or even watched.

Then, the realisation that if my abuser did this so blatantly in front of my friend. How could the adults or other people in my life not hear or see what was happening? It also makes me wonder if other kids saw what was happening and were talking about it. Or did some kids have similar abuse occurring in their own homes?

Then I remembered there was another occurrence that happened in front of someone. It was our neighbour, a boy about five years older than me. They had moved in after my grandparents sold the house next door to us. My abuser decided to do something sexual to me in front of this boy. It felt at the time like my abuser was showing off! Strange as that may sound.

Then my abuser pushed me towards the neighbour and motioned – your turn!

This was the first house I lived in. So, I know I was around eight years old when the new neighbours lived next door. It was not long after that we moved to our second house.

Luckily for me, the boy next door looked disgusted. This humiliated me at the time, which is why I remember this instance so well.

After I had confided in my dad as an adult, about what happened to me, my dad then brought this instance up to my abuser when he confronted them with my abuse, to which my abuser pleaded ignorance.

Imagine if the neighbour had decided to take it further with me!

I want to know what else I have buried. **What else was there that my little body and mind were subjected to? Was I just a guinea pig to experiment on?** I believe I must have taken my mind off to another place during some of my abuse. The reason I want to know is because each time I find out something else that happened, I have to work through this extra trauma again. I need to get it all out so I can heal more.

I've learnt over the years that some parents may even allow their children to be in harmful situations, because they themselves were not protected as children.

This was astounding to me when my psychologist brought this up during one of our sessions. Because I have gone the complete opposite way with my children. Being overprotective and overly sensitive to any potential threats to their health or safety.

There are a lot of famous people who have tried to help stop child abuse or bring it to the public's awareness over the years also. Lots of celebrities that you wouldn't think, have had terrible things happen to them as children, and most often don't speak about it until they are adults. But it is a powerful thing for people in the public eye or spotlight to talk about these matters, due to the influence they have on everyday people.

Trauma Bonding

Sinead O'Connor who you may know from her song – "Nothing Compares To You" - who passed away recently, was one person who tried her best to bring child sexual abuse into the light, to help stop it from continuing. I recently watched an interview she did with Dr Phil, and it was very confronting to watch.

What I got from watching this interview was her extreme trauma bonding with her mum, who was her abuser. Sinead struggled with how she felt about her mum at different times in her life. This is a very good example of trauma bonding and all the strong, confusing emotions we all feel due to the person who hurt us being a significant member of our family. Especially being the closest female, a girl has in her life. That same sex parent is the most influential role model and are the ones who help shape how we deal with our relationships, behaviours and decision making as we grow up.

During her interview with Dr Phil, I saw how proud and confident Sinead became when speaking about her music career. She knew how good she was as an artist, and it seemed to be her safe and healing place when she sang. She explained how she wrote about her trauma in some of her songs, like a diary of a person recovering from child abuse. I can relate to this as I feel the same about writing my poems.

I was asked recently who I wanted to emulate, and this is who. Sinead O'Connor is my hero, for what she did by standing up and trying to help other child sexual abuse victims during her life.

Ways in which you can break a trauma bond with a parent –

- Communicate your needs clearly and assertively
- Remove yourself from the situation – disengage from the person
- Come to terms with your feelings
- Validate yourself
- Find resources or professionals to assist you

- Write down or journal your feelings
- Find a purpose or project to occupy your time
- Stop blaming yourself
- Prioritise yourself and your wants and needs
- Take time to grieve what you've lost

Remember a trauma bond is formed when you find comfort from the person who has hurt you or let you down when you were a child. Or left you unprotected when young. There will usually be a very strong connection between yourself and this person and this will be a difficult bond to break. So, finding the right resources and assistance in this process is paramount to you being able to break these harmful patterns that have been formed throughout your life, once and for all.

Strength Struck

If I had had the chance to meet Sinead O'Connor, I wouldn't be "Star Struck" but "Strength Struck." Her strength as a person, rather than as an artist, is what I would be overwhelmed to know all about. We should be struck by the strength of the average person rather than all these celebrities that people look up to. I realise actors, singers, athletes, etc., all work hard to get to where they are. But so does the young man who serves you at the bakery, with the warm smile he shows you, even though he's always struggled socially. Or the old man who went to war to fight for his country, who helps his neighbour who's a single mum and can't fix her broken door. The woman doing your facial that you use as a sounding board with all your problems. Who is just trying to get through each day herself.

Or the cashier who's been on their feet all day and has to deal with your bad mood when you knock off from work. But still smiles at you and does their job professionally.

Anyone who can put their problems aside to help you or stands up to people doing the wrong things, are the real heroes in life, and you should be struck by the strength of these people.

I found you that day

It began, much like any other day,
You came, to give some gifts away,
You had no idea, what was to come,
I struggled to say, what I had to mum.

You looked at me, like a scared little kid,
But I had to tell you, just what they did,
We'd both been protecting, our mother's son,
You knew deep down, just what they'd done.

I'd tried for years, to save you this grief,
But pushing it down, couldn't change my belief,
You knew in your heart, this day would come,
I struggled to say, what I had to mum.

You told me no, then you turned to leave,
Your eyes showed, you didn't want to believe,
It was them or me, and you chose them again,
Unfortunately, I had become used to this pain.

The tears keep coming, but you'll never know,
It hurts so much, but I try hard not to show,
I've got to be strong, for the ones to come,
I struggled to say, what I had to mum.

So, I lost you that day, my beautiful mum,
But I had to, just so that I could become,
The person I'd lost, so many years ago,
Cause without loss, we never really grow.

Then I found you that day, girl I should have been,
Through the hurt and the pain, you'll finally be seen,
Though I'll never be whole, not from that moment on,
Bridges need to be crossed; journeys must be begun.

Chapter 24

Can't get off the roundabout

If the survivor has lived with a family member who abused them, or the bystander who didn't help them (their whole life), or they have gone back home time and time again, they may find it nearly impossible to move on without these people.

As I spoke about in Chapter 23 about trauma bonding, the survivor becomes attached to their abuser or bystander in an unhealthy way and cannot easily break free.

Even though it is a mental hell and torment living as an adult with their abuser or supposed protector/bystander, they don't feel strong enough to pull away. They have been mentally beaten down so much over the years that trying to live on their own is very scary to them. The unknown feels worse than what they know because of their low self-esteem and lack of confidence. Other healthy individuals develop resilience and confidence during their childhood/teens and early 20s, but a sexual abuse survivor who hasn't had those milestones may be unable to help themselves get free later in life.

If a survivor is given all the resources, such as psychiatrists, psychologists, community domestic violence contacts, refuges to stay at, government payments and ongoing assistance to start their life elsewhere. They may turn them all down in order to return to the home they are being tormented in. The abuse may have stopped years ago, but the trauma is still felt each and every day they stay around these toxic people.

The survivor may sabotage any help offered by others. Every excuse under the sun may be used to find a way not to accept this help. This must frustrate people like psychologists, psychiatrists and social workers. You can lead a horse to water, but you can't make it drink. This saying goes for traumatised people, too, and it won't make sense to most people. But, hopefully, by now, you should have a better understanding, as I do, of why fractured people are like this. I only wish there was a way we could make them see how different and better their lives would be once they were free of their current circumstances.

In my final Chapter 35 – Give me your hand, so I can push you back down. You will see just how hard it can be to pull away from the people who have tried to persuade you to keep quiet all your life. Sometimes, our family members will have used quite subtle forms of manipulation, and you won't even realise it has happened until you get older and look back. Some of our family may have been very vocal and forthright in controlling us, and some may have used much more understated ways to manipulate us into silence.

So, whether it is a stab directly in the back or death by a thousand cuts, it will have the same effect of keeping us quiet. **If we continue to let them!!!!**

You'll See Their Strength One Day

The little girl, you saw as weak,
The boy, who had no strength to speak,
The lad, who knew not what to say,
Just wait, you'll see their strength one day.

The one, who had to bite their tongue,
The child who froze, and couldn't run,
While screaming, in their head for mum,
Their fight and justice, still to come.

So, you were big, and they were small,
What made you think, to make that call,
The choice to rip, away their tomorrow,
Now nothing's left, but tears and sorrow.

Did you feel strong, and in control,
While their smiles, and voices you stole,
One day, we'll see the tables turn,
And justice, is a thing YOU'LL learn.

That bikie dude, who just rode in,
Tats galore, and a huge, big grin,
You don't know him, now that he's grown,
And now, he's got YOU all alone!

That girl who sidles up to, the bar,
Inside, she hides one unhealed scar,
No more ribbons, or pigtails in her hair,
She's looking now, to make things square.

How does it feel, now they are big,
Now they could snap you, like a twig,
I'm sure your stomach's, in your throat,
We'd all love to be there, just to gloat!

This poem is for all the abusers,
Written on behalf of the accusers,
One day, we'll find a way to heal,
No longer ruled, by our ordeal

Chapter 25

No good deed goes unpunished

You can't stay where you are, if you want things to change

Have you ever been torn between telling a friend something difficult or not saying anything at all?

Say you find out your best friend's boyfriend is cheating on them. You know it will hurt them badly, but you are also stuck knowing this information now. So, what do you do?

Example 1. - You tell them. This can be hard, but you feel they should know, as you would want to know if your boyfriend was cheating on you.

But......... then you become the messenger, and this can lead to a lot of issues. They may decide they don't want to know and bury their head in the sand. The boyfriend now dislikes you for telling on him. Your friend decides she wants to stay with him, cheater or not. Where does this leave you? You become an outcast to them as it doesn't suit either of them that you know the secret. You lose a friend all because you did what you thought was the right thing to do.

Example 2. – You don't tell your friend her boyfriend is cheating on her. Then your friend finds out some other way and also finds out you knew and didn't tell her! Now you are in trouble because of what you didn't do!

The reason I am giving these examples is because sometimes in life, you just can't win. No matter what you do, it's the wrong thing in some people's eyes. And this is because they can't deal with the position they are in.

This happens with intra-familial childhood sexual abuse survivors, too.

When trying to help someone who has been traumatised by sexual abuse as a child, you will come up against a lot of issues that you could never have predicted. It is such a complex, confusing, and confronting issue, and you can never foresee how someone will react.

I have written below some examples of how this could play out.

1. You know what happened. How do you talk to them about what happened if they aren't ready to divulge this information? It can be a very tricky thing to navigate. No doubt there will be denial, at least at first. It is very scary to find out that someone else knows about it since they are still holding onto the secret so tightly. They may pull away from you and distance themselves even though you are only trying to help them. What you are dealing with is a fractured individual who doesn't react or think like you due to their trauma. You may have to be patient and give them space until they are ready to come back to you. They may never be ready. On the other hand, they may feel relief that they can now talk to someone who understands and is willing to help them.

2. The conversation - You will have to be very gentle and choose your words carefully. Let them do most of the talking. Saying things like - you just have to move on, etc., is not ok to say to an abuse survivor. This will trigger them and make them feel as though you don't understand, and then they will feel isolated all over again. Suggest counselling or just be there when they want to talk to you.

3. Consequences to the perpetrator – No doubt there will be a conversation about their perpetrator and how they feel about pressing charges or not. As it is a family member this can be very tricky. All the emotions are heightened since someone close to them did this to them. They will be going through a myriad of feelings about this.

4. Ongoing help – Since you are now the only one they can rely on a great deal of pressure will be on you. You will have to be careful you don't betray their trust, even if you think you are doing the right thing. Telling them it isn't their secret will be helpful. They need to realise this was done to them, not by them, in any way. Abuse survivors will always find a way to make themselves feel guilty about their childhood abuse. It's just what we do. Education and counselling will help them realise it wasn't their fault and that they aren't responsible for whatever consequences happen to their perpetrator, if they choose to seek consequences or even just speak their truth to other family members.

5. Extended family – The next step will be talking to their other family members, about what happened to them. This could go 1 of 2 ways. They may be believed and receive love and support from their family. Or their family may refuse to believe them, and they will be rejected. **This will probably be the hardest stage in this whole process.**

6. No good deed goes unpunished – What happens if they don't get the result they want or were hoping for? You may become the bad guy. They listened to you and look where it got them. Their family has turned against them. You need to be very aware of this outcome before entering this situation. Because it can happen, and I know this all too well. All the help, resources and kindness you have given them could all be turned against you very quickly if their family does not believe them or they don't get the result they were hoping for.

As mentioned earlier, some survivors may self-sabotage at times. Because, just like my example at the beginning of this chapter, you never know how someone is going to react. Particularly when they have been hurt so much in their life, and the easiest target may be you. This is because you have shown them kindness and care, which can be the direction their frustration takes. Especially if they have mental health issues already. Even the fact that they may be trauma-bonded to the person who hurt them or their supposed protector. Which may make it impossible for them to leave the family fold. This may seem to them to be the easiest place to stay. But it is plain to see from the outside that staying where they are is not a good environment for them and very unhealthy for their mental and physical wellbeing.

Chapter 26

Chop down your family tree

Some people's families are so toxic, that they don't deserve to even be called a family.

An abusive family does not make a home, and your biggest inner conflict may be how you feel about your family.

One of the things people say that makes me really angry is. "Oh, but they're your family." No, not if they treat you badly, they're not. Take the label (mother, father, brother, etc.) off these people and see if you would accept the same treatment from strangers.

Or – "You can't turn your back on your family!" Why not? They've turned their back on you by being abusive, toxic and hurting you. What is worse than intra-familial childhood sexual abuse? How can we stand to still see our family members, if they were involved in, or knew and did nothing, about this most heinous of crimes committed against us as children?

How can your family not consider sexual abuse a crime? If you were shot, stabbed, choked or struck with an object, it is a crime and charges are laid. Why, then, if you abuse a child sexually in the family home, is it not taken seriously? The hurt, fear and mental torture remain long after the physical scars from the crimes mentioned above would have healed.

There seem to be so many people who fight against you to keep the "sick secrets" hidden and, therefore, continuing in families like their life depends on it. And this is the selfish reality of abusers and bystanders. They only look at themselves and see how this will affect them if it's found out. They can't seem to see how it affects US! Or how our quality of life later, depends on them doing the right thing when we are young. OUR LIFE has meaning, too, and any other victim of a crime would be helped, not shunned.

So clearly, if the "wagons" are circling the secret/perpetrator. Then where else can we be but on the outside alone, under attack and feeling helpless?

They say you teach people how to treat you, but I disagree with that to some extent. I think our experiences in childhood teach us, which include how our families or abusers made us feel and moulded us as children, as to how we are treated later in life. Then we just continue on these sometimes destructive pathways. Allowing people to treat us badly in the future. **So, for us as adult survivors, we need to rewrite our future by discontinuing to lean into these same harmful behaviours and take a different fork in the road.**

If people continue along these lines of "That's just the way it is" then nothing will ever change, and history has shown us that we need to change to make progress as human beings. Don't let them tell you to be quiet! Just because that's how it's always been done in the past generations. **That silence is the very reason you are now struggling with your own childhood sexual abuse trauma! Because those who came before you didn't speak up!**

You need to surround yourself with people who charge your batteries, not drain them.

Just because you were born into a family does not mean you are born of that family. By this, I mean you don't always have the same mentality, morals or behaviours as your family members, and you have a choice to participate in their ways when you become an adult.

My biggest confusion has been how I feel about my family. I no longer see my family member who abused me, and my relationship with my supposed protector hangs by a thread, just waiting for the wrong thing to be said again. This is the upsetting truth of how abuse not dealt with plays out within families. It needn't be this way if people tell the truth and help the victims/survivors.

So, I suppose the question remains to be asked. Are these people who have hurt you or let you down monsters to the general population? Or have they been to you your whole life? Probably not in the whole scheme of things, no. They are your average people on the street who may help the old lady across the road or give donations to charity. They have probably helped you out during your life too, seeing they are your family members. This is what makes what happened to us so disabling and damaging at times, because you keep going back and forth in your mind about what happened and also what part they may have played in your life after the abuse.

This is why it took me 44 years to remove myself from my situation, because I kept giving my abuser another chance and trying to block out what they did to me. And giving my bystander the benefit of the doubt. My bystander/supposed protector, in particular, has helped me in a lot of ways throughout my life. There is no doubt about that. They are not evil. They have just not had the backbone to hold my abuser to account or show me the respect I deserved, which has had a flow-on effect on our relationship. So, I suppose what I am trying to say and explain here is that the back and forth in my mind and other survivors' minds will be exhausting, confusing and totally disconcerting throughout our lives, which would not have taken place if our abusers were not our family members. Because then the right healing processes to assist us would have been facilitated when we were young.

I have seen this same emotional turmoil play out in other types of abusive situations. When a parent has murdered the other parent of a child, the child will feel so conflicted because they loved both of their parents. They will miss the one who is gone but also have a strange bond with their other parent. This seems messed up, but it is just how our minds and hearts work and react. Once again we go back and forth with our emotions about this person who has hurt us so deeply. But at other times they have been there for us. It's psychologically exhausting, and no one wins being the victim in these kinds of situations.

I have personally told my children and husband that I don't want what I have been subjected to or am dealing with to affect their relationships with these people. This is my journey, not theirs. Being family members, they have also grown up with them. So, that is a decision they need to make for themselves, and I am not asking them to take sides.

One thing I want to point out also is the ramifications that our abuse can have on the partners we pick later in life. My husband had a good idea there was something wrong before I told him about what happened to me. This was due to him having a previous girlfriend who had been abused, and he could see similar signs in me too. Then, after I let him know about my abuse, I also muted him from saying or doing anything against my abuser. This put a huge strain on him having to be around this person, who did so much harm to me as a child and the trauma that carried on throughout my adult life also. My relationship with my husband was affected in so many ways. One of which was my shame around sex at times, and he knew who was to blame for this and had to be around this person on occasion. I realise now it was unfair of me to do this, but I still felt muted myself when I first let him in on what had happened to me. At this time, I didn't feel like I could make waves in the family. I was still scared and holding on to the secret so tightly. **Until I finally worked out it wasn't mine to hold on to.**

I recently took part in a University research survey for child abuse victims. As part of this survey, they asked me what services were provided to me as a child to help me. I told them none. Absolutely zero! Because my abuse happened in the family home, it was covered up. So, I wasn't given the chance or choice to receive ongoing help or resources.

Someone said to me you don't know what it's like to feel abandoned because your family have always been there for you as a kid. I said there is a difference between someone physically being there compared to someone emotionally being there.

Childhood sexual abuse isn't something that everyone knows about or how to deal with. But just like if your child had diabetes or another illness or health issue, it's up to the parent/caregiver to educate themselves on how to help their child when they are young.

Why is sexual abuse any different in some people's eyes? It's still a health issue, both physically and mentally. Why didn't my supposed protector step up and find out how to help me? This is what I mean about being emotionally there for me.

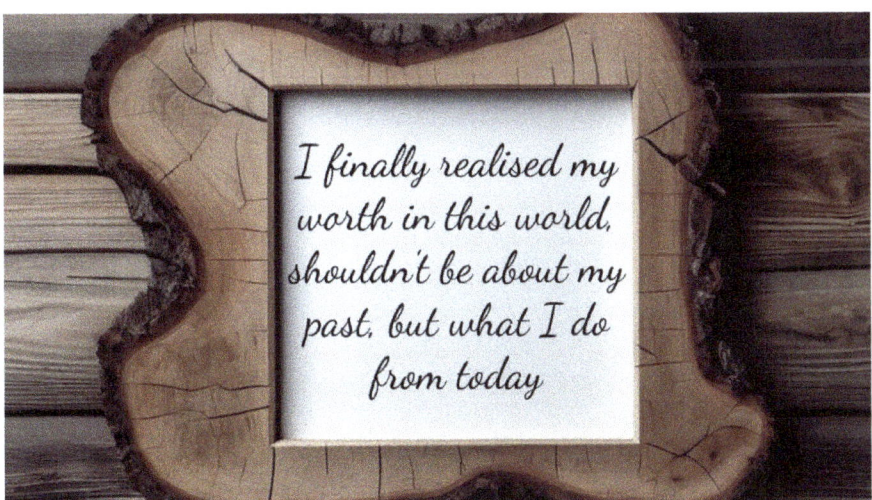

You Don't Want To Be Me!

Posters are up, there's a sight to be seen,
The carnival is here, and this time it is free!
Roll up, roll up if you've never been,
No money is needed, but there's always a fee.

The circle of wagons stops in a new town,
1800's entertainment for all you good folks,
Susie runs to her mum; can we go see the clowns?
Everyone loves a clown, so there's no need to coax.

Susie glances back to look at the banner,
But what she sees makes her stop in her tracks,
She pulls her mum's arm and begins to st-st-stammer,
The posters now blank, so she tries to turn back.

Our main attractions tonight, for all you kind folks,
Bearded lady, who hides her secrets so well,
Invisible perps, you can just see their cloaks,
The caged victim, high up there in their cell.

Don't tarry or you will miss all the freaks,
The knife thrower – no, don't turn your back!
The bystander, who will just never speak,
The fact juggler, watch them slip through the crack.

Also appearing tonight in our small town,
The trapeze artists, see they always bounce back,
And of course, there's always the family of clowns,
For anyone who knows better, it's all just bushwhack.

Tonight, for your pleasure, will you please welcome sir,
The geriatric Nay Sayers, they are easy to find,
And last but not least while you're still in a blur,
The extended family of the deaf, dumb and blind.

The tent starts to fill up with excited young kids,
They see glitter and glamour, a sight to behold,
But it's all smoke and mirrors, a true age-old fib,
The horrors to come, are at this stage untold.

It's all a mistake, please oh please, you must leave,
Susie cries out to the crowd, no there's nothing to see,
But the attractions are too good, they don't want to believe,
To her friends, she says stop! You don't want to be me!

Little Susie walks in, and stops dead in her tracks,
Mother drags her along, sits her down on her lap,
She covers her eyes, and tries to face back,
All these mystical creatures, the crowd starts to clap.

The performers all focus their eyes on one child,
They know she sees them, for what they really are,
They look at each other, oh no this is not good!
They see now, she's grown very strong from her scars.

The ringmaster announces - fun for the whole family!
For 100's of years, we've kept this secret padlocked,
His performance deserves an award, from the academy,
But Susie the victim just stares and says -WHAT?

The monsters on stage, are still wearing their masks,
The crowd starts to whisper, they are all in a daze,
And the parents and children are still yet to grasp,
Only Susie can see, they are trapped in a haze.

We need a volunteer from the audience please,
A little girl, 2nd row stands up to be picked,
The trauma in Susie is making her freeze,
Then she snaps out of it and screams no – it's a trick!

Something in her scream, makes the audience turn round,
When they turn back they see, that there's really no clowns,
No glitter, no glamour, no fun to be found,
Just monsters and evil, they all slowly drown!

But mum is still smiling, what's going on here?
Susie removes mum's rose-coloured glasses, to see,
Slowly but slowly, mum screams out in fear,
Susie's strength in herself, has finally set her mum free.

Came over the tent, an immediate hush,
This age-old attraction, no longer a thrill,
Then all of a sudden, there was such a rush,
Clambering to escape, someone could have been killed.

Mum looks at her Susie, says how could I not see?
It's ok now mum, I've brought them out of the dark,
Now all the other young children, can also be free,
But the journey from here mum, I must alone embark.

Susie turns around, and strikes at a match,
Throws it into the tent, where the monsters are trapped,
Hoping beyond hope, that the fabric will catch,
And this generational story, can at last be unwrapped.

But for all the good in the world, there's always been evil,
And I know better than most, just where it's been hiding,
So, it's unsurprising for me, to find this upheaval,
One monster unseen, slips out through the tents siding.

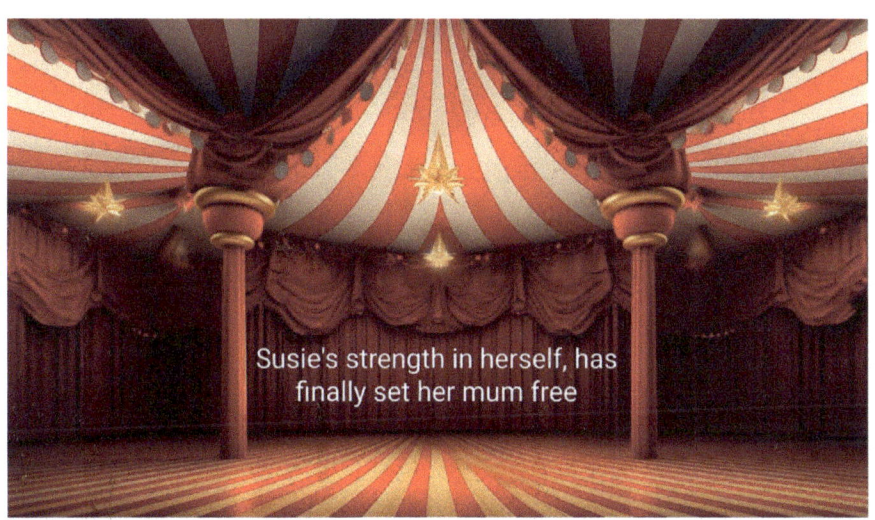

Chapter 27

Eyes wide shut

Eye's wide shut meaning - what is hidden in plain sight, and we chose not to see.

Looking back, my abuse became apparent when I was about eight or nine years old, (fourth grade). Signs that anyone who had been paying attention would have noticed - stomach issues regularly at school, with lots of visits to the nurse's room. Easily triggered fight or flight response, especially when my supposed protector would drop me off somewhere. Or high anxiety if doing something new. Clinging to my supposed protector and not wanting them to leave me. Crying when left at night with babysitters. Not wanting my supposed protector to drive, especially when raining, as I was terrified they would die in a car accident. Trouble sleeping over at friends' houses later on and avoiding school. These are just a handful of things.

You see, my supposed protector was my safe person back then. They could do no wrong in my young eyes. They were someone I thought would never let me down. They were the one I first confided in about my abuse when I was maybe ten or eleven years old.

By the time I started high school in Sydney (year seven), I was a mess.

Primary school had been hard enough, but high school was even worse. Another unknown experience that triggered my anxiety. New friends to make, new classes, new teachers and new routines.

I tried to hide it from my peers, but every day was a struggle for me and having some boys give me a hard time at school didn't help either. I'm sure those boys would feel terrible now, if they knew just how hard I had it back then.

So, there was no place I felt safe or could relax. Not at home or school. It just shows you can never really know what someone is going through.

I clearly remember getting ready for high school one day, and my dad was going to drop me off that morning. My dad had no idea what was happening. I said I had to go upstairs for something, but he knew me too well and wasn't letting me go back up. I had tried to skip school so many times before, with excuses like illness, etc..

I tried to run past him, and he dragged me down the stairs, yelling that he was going to call an ambulance to take me to the mental hospital as he was tired of me trying to get out of school and couldn't understand why I was acting this way. This should have been a huge red flag to my dad that something was very wrong. But this was in the 1980s, and this kind of thing wasn't thought about or discussed. If only my supposed protector had told him what was going on back then!

I feel a great loss and sadness because I lost the special relationship a daughter should have with her father growing up due to the abuse I was suffering from at home. I became scared of males when I was little, and I used to get in trouble for saying "Shut up" to men who said anything about my appearance, such as "What a pretty little girl." Something in me didn't like male attention, even at such a young age. I was fearful of males, and I also didn't take any kind of compliments well due to my feeling of never being good enough. So, I found it very hard to understand why someone was praising me. I had so much doubt in myself and wondered what they wanted from me.

So, just like in the chapter about – The Ongoing Hurt – my childhood relationship with my dad is just more collateral damage from my abuse.

When I was in grade eight, my supposed protector did work at my high school. Some kind of help in a resources area, so they could stay at school with me, just to get me to go each day. Which, of course, I felt bad about making them do. Due to my circumstances, I could easily make my life a living hell without anyone else's help. By then, I'd been programmed to feel confusion, guilt and shame from a very young age.

When I was in grade nine, we moved to a different state. I somehow developed a way to compartmentalise my life and what had happened to me. Pushed the memories down, so to speak, and tried to reinvent myself.

I have been able to put what happened out of my mind at lots of different times during my life. But not forever.

Around the age of sixteen, I left school and started working. I also started drinking and going to clubs. Not coming home and basically looking for trouble. As I was troubled! Rebelling against all the rules I'd been given as a child and finally acting out.

In my late teens and 20s, I looked for love and validation wherever I could find it. I was attracted to men who were big and muscular. I thought they were strong and could protect me. But the strength I needed was not in a physical form. The strength I longed for was someone who would treat me well, with kindness, comfort, and support.

I became a single mum at nineteen and let myself be disrespected over and over again by men. Because I just wanted someone to love, take care of me and not leave. But what I was getting was more men just using and abusing me due to my false interpretation of what love was. I was easily manipulated because that was what I was used to. So, I accepted less than my worth. A lot of abuse survivors will have abandonment issues. They will try to hold on to their partner, even if that partner is not good for them, as I did.

When I was in my 20s, still a single mum, I was working in the office at one of three timber mills I was employed at over the years. I worked three days a week when my son was a toddler. I met one of the people who would become one of my great friends to this day. She told me years later that I had always seemed so anxious, like an energiser bunny, just going and going. I had no idea people could see my anxiety. I was under the illusion that I hid it well. Apparently not!

By the time I was in my late 20s or early 30s, I began to start to question how males had treated me in the past. The anger started to rise in me when I felt used sexually. I started to see I wasn't being my true self and questioned who I was, and **what did I want?** Rather than just what was expected of me. Up until then, I had just let males control me and tell me what to do, what to wear, and how to act. So, in many ways, I didn't think for myself.

I had a breakdown when I was about thirty-two. We had been living in a small house that we were renovating. I was not taking care of my health, and I was just going and going to block out the pain. The trigger was my current home life, but it wasn't the cause. The cause was my childhood abuse not being dealt with and all the trauma responses I had put into place during my life, which were unhealthy for me.

Everything came crashing down one night when it all got too much for me, and I sat on the kitchen floor and sobbed. No one knew what to do. I was having a panic attack and didn't realise what was happening. Except that I felt like I couldn't breathe. My eldest son read me a book to take my mind off it. He was so sweet. My husband then took me to the hospital as I thought it was my asthma, but it was instead my first panic attack. But unfortunately, it wouldn't be my last. This was a really scary time for me, and I didn't want to be left alone with my young daughter, who was only a toddler due to the fact that my panic attacks made me feel like I was dying and out of control. I couldn't even drive my older sons to school anymore and didn't want any social contact as it was just too stressful being around people. I was scared I would make a fool out of myself at any given time.

I went to stay with my supposed protector for a week. I cried continuously and lost a lot of weight, as I couldn't eat due to the severe emotional breakdown I was having. I realise now that at that time, I was trauma-bonded because I found comfort in the person who was supposed to protect me as a child but didn't.

After speaking with my doctor and being put on antidepressants, the panic attacks finally stopped, and I was able to take care of my family again and socialise. You see, my trauma response was and still is, to some extent, to not stop. So I don't have to think about things that are too hard to deal with. And the reason I ended up having this huge breakdown was because I hadn't dealt with my abuse. But just continued to try and push it down. **But that rubber ducky just won't stay under the water!**

Things got really bad for me again during my early 40s, which is when I stopped seeing my abuser who had hurt me as a child.

I found it very hard to be around my parents at this time in my life. They had moved their van to our place, in-between buying a house, and I had to see them every day. It was too much of a trigger for me, and things got very bad between us. They didn't understand what was happening, so I sat them down and spoke to them about what had happened to me when I was little. My supposed protector had not told my dad and he was shocked. He went white as a ghost as all the blood drained from his face. He didn't speak to my supposed protector for two weeks. He was so angry at them for not letting him know what happened when I was a child. This made me feel guilty. It was just so ingrained in me back then to feel guilt when I see someone else in pain. Even though logically, I understand that none of this is my fault.

Now I'm fifty and finally able to put down all my feelings and experiences on paper. I can see so clearly now all the chapters in my life and the processes one has to go through to get to a better place. The seasons in our lives are there for a reason. Good or bad, we need to understand the lessons life throws our way and grow from them.

Chapter 28
Plants - an Analogy

While working in my garden, I came to realise that people are very much like flowers and plants. Some of my plants grew well in full sun, while others couldn't stand the heat and needed more shade. Some liked lots of water, while others died when given the same amount of water. Some grew strong and tall. But others were bending or growing in strange directions and needed a splint to help them stand up straight.

People are just like plants in this regard. Especially childhood sexual abuse survivors. Everyone is so different in how they have dealt with their trauma. Some of us block it out. Some have grown to hate. Some have become very empathetic. Some self-harm. Some have developed mental illness. Some are workaholics and don't sit still. Some have addictions. Some have OCD. Some have become trauma-bonded, and some sadly have lost their lives. But also, some have found strength from their pain, helping others, and are blossoming! This could be you, too!

When I was a little girl, my nanna had the most beautiful flower gardens, and she used to let me help her water them. One of the first lessons I learned was that you don't water the tops of the flowers, as I naively thought, but you must water the base to get the water to the roots. This is the same with abuse survivors. You can't deal with the surface stuff; you have to get to the root of the problem, go deep, to truly help them.

In a garden, you also have to deadhead/cut off the old flowers so the rest of the plant can thrive. Otherwise, the plant will struggle and sometimes die. This is the same with our trauma and also our family members, who aren't helpful. They can weigh us down and not allow us to live our best lives because we carry too much baggage.

Then, there are weeds to pull out in every garden. As with the people we surround ourselves with, we need to keep the plants but remove the weeds. **Only keep the people who are good for you, and then your garden will be beautiful and healthy, and so will you.**

Circling the wagons

I am the tree, they tried to cut down,
Not with an axe, but just with a frown.
Was treated like a guest, in my own home,
Illusions of childhood, now all that I own.

Each year that went by, a little more disappears,
Our shadows grow tall, but we retreat in our fears,
Hiding under the covers, scared to open our eyes,
Sitting here doing time, while they live out their lies.

It wasn't our secret, but the shame weighed us down,
As Barbara Streisand says – send in the clowns!
Can't you see where all here Barbs, too many to count,
Telling truth through our stories, only way we surmount.

Generational mistakes, look away, look away,
Trapped in a snow globe, with nothing to say,
Now we are the scapegoats on the family tree,
Standing up for each other, only way to be free.

While they circle their wagons, we must all stay outside,
Keeping ancient secrets safe, our shame we do hide,
But who built the wagons, the wagon maker did,
From the wagon maker, I tried to hide as a kid.

In The Wizard of Oz, there was a message for us,
Glinda the good witch, says one thing you should trust,
You've always had the power my dear, you just had to learn for yourself,
Click those ruby slippers three times, this chapter belongs on the shelf.

But just like the Lorax, did speak for the trees,
Now it's my turn, to help others be free,
So, give me your hand, I will help you get through,
One day at a time, we have so much to do.

Chapter 29

Kaleidoscope

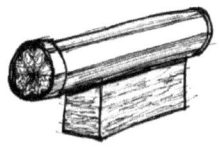

A kaleidoscope has a constantly changing pattern.

Kaleidoscopes that you have as a child have beautiful colours and patterns.

Love from a family member that is not right is very similar. Except for the part about it being beautiful, it is anything but. When I say love I speak from the child's point of view. This isn't love. It is sexual abuse. But the child thinks of it as love because they don't know any better or different at this point in their young, innocent lives.

What I want to try to explain in this chapter is how a child feels with these conflicted emotions from their abuse from a trusted and loved family member, when they are young, compared to when they grow up.

It is a challenging and complex experience to try to explain to someone who has not had it happen to them. One that even the abuse survivor will struggle to understand their whole life. So, I'll try to make this as clear as possible.

When a child experiences attention, affection or someone telling them they are special, loved, etc., in an abusive situation, they think this feeling is normal and right. They don't know any better because they are just innocent and vulnerable children, and this is their reality at the time.

Like a kaleidoscope, a pattern forms in a child's mind and life. But this pattern is everchanging and one that when the child grows up and realises how wrong it all was, will become especially distressing and mentally disturbing to them. This is because they will feel they participated willingly. That is not the case! As described in Chapter 4 – Consent or the lack thereof.

Another reason childhood sexual abuse is so heinous and mentally distressing is that the child may actually feel pleasure while the abuse is happening. The child becomes sexualised during their abuse, and maybe the only way I can explain this to someone who hasn't experienced it is like being tickled. Or when you are a kid and someone draws on your back, brushes your hair, etc., It awakens these senses in you.

Your body will have an automatic response to what's happening to you. Once again, I will remind you, that the child knows no better at their age. So, they don't realise this is wrong and not normal.

This is why when we become adults and remember what happened and how we felt and reacted, we are so conflicted and ashamed of our body's response when we were little. We will beat ourselves up mentally and feel disgusted with ourselves, when we should be kind and take it easy on ourselves, because we were just naive and blameless children at the time.

We knew no better. Could not get out of the situation we were in. **Due to the control our perpetrator had over us and our vulnerability due to our age and were ultimately "abused."**

"Abused meaning" – use or treat in such a way as to cause damage or harm.

Example – It's like watching animals get tricked into traps with food in them. And that's just an illustration of how, as kids, we couldn't see the harm coming our way, while we were young.

When I hear about child sexual abuse victims committing suicide when they are adults. It makes me so very angry and sad, that they couldn't get to a point in their lives where they didn't blame themselves and were so mentally tormented that they weren't able to continue to live with this anguish and hurt.

This pain cuts very deep and continues during a survivor's life in so many other distressing and damaging ways. So many health issues come from our abuse, as mentioned earlier. I have struggled my whole life with conditions such as IBS (irritable bowel syndrome) from the abuse I experienced, due to the way my mind and body have now become overreactive as part of my trauma. The enteric nervous system that regulates our gut is often referred to as the body's second brain, which is why I have this reaction.

Trauma can switch your body's stress response into high gear for the rest of your life. Medical issues such as autoimmune diseases can occur from abuse as a child. I have also had other medical issues, such as arthritis in my hands, much earlier than would be expected. (An autoimmune condition). A tumour in my appendix a couple of years ago, and I have been under the care of several specialists for other health issues that have arisen as I've gotten older.

Childhood trauma is also linked to an increased risk of other numerous health problems such as -

- Cancer
- Stroke

- Obesity
- Diabetes
- Heart disease

This is because the chronic stress we feel from our trauma elevates levels of stress hormones in our bodies over our lifetime, which takes its toll as we age.

Ways in which we can help to alleviate our health issues -

Meditation – I have found doing meditation every day is such a huge benefit to my stress and anxiety levels. The breathing techniques shown in the app I use help me to breathe deeper and slower and get my body to relax. Also listening to affirmations during these sessions is very helpful to get my mind clearer and feel better about myself.

Meditation also allows you to live in the present moment rather than worry about the future.

Some meditation apps have gentle rain, etc. or background music to breathe to and stories to listen to when you're struggling to sleep. Or to just enjoy at any time.

Exercise – exercise is a great way to get the stress and tightness out of your body that builds up due to your trauma. Walking is the way I keep fit, and I also enjoy listening to music while I walk. This is my time, and finding some time for yourself each day is very important. Doing Pilates also helps me loosen up my tight muscles, and lifting weights is a great stress reliever.

Read or listen – get engrossed in a good novel or biography. Listen to a podcast about something you enjoy or can learn from. **Be inspired by others and grow.**

Chapter 30
Age is no defence

Whether you are a child abuse survivor, bystander or the perpetrator, age is no defence.

The perpetrator

Just because perpetrators may be old now, there is no reason for them not to be held to account for what they did. Being old doesn't take away from the crime they committed against a child. **It just means they have gotten away with it their whole life, while you have been living a life sentence, when it should have been THEM doing time.**

I have heard of a father who molested his child, and the child pressed charges when they were an adult. The father actually admitted to what he did, pleaded guilty and did some jail time. I think this is the only way any survivor will get a tiny sense of peace from what was done to them, if any peace is ever to be had.

It takes guts for a perpetrator to say what they did, especially to their own flesh and blood. That's why most offenders will always deny what they did. So, there will very rarely be an admission of guilt from your abuser or a sorry. **Therefore, you must not wait for this outcome**

to help yourself. You do not need their admission to know what happened……. **you know!**

The bystander

Once again, age doesn't make it ok for the bystander not to be held accountable. They let you down and have kept the "sick secret" to protect the perpetrator, which some may say is just as bad as the act itself. The fact that the person who is meant to protect you has abandoned you to protect the person who hurt you, is indefensible.

The bystander, in many cases, may have also suffered abuse as a child and have not dealt with their trauma. They may have blocked it out and aren't able to handle it. So therefore, they can't grasp what happened to you either, and they just want you to do the same. Or they may have also told their parent and were silenced or not helped. **But as I continue to say, not dealing with abuse helps no one and just carries it on down to the next generation.**

But our generation is a lot stronger than theirs. We know more, and I'm hoping we will do more for our kids. Not to mention ourselves. The strength I've seen with the "Me too" movement in my children's generation has made me even prouder as a human being. Because I also had older men in work situations, etc., take advantage of me as a young woman. I was too shy or uncomfortable at the time to stand up for myself, particularly when I was made to feel like my job was on the line if I spoke up.

The child abuse survivor

No matter how old you are, if you are an abuse survivor, you have every right to take your power back. I don't care if you're 80, 90 or 100! We all need to find the strength to tell our story and find our peace, even if your abuser is no longer alive, you can tell your loved ones your story. You may even help someone else in your family find the courage to speak up.

When I showed my current psychologist some of my poems and read him my book, he told me it was very brave of me to do this. I told him I don't really see myself as brave. It's just something I feel needs to be done. But after that, I partially agreed with him that the very personal information I have written about was hard to put down on paper.

But then again, I know it was done to me, not by me and that I was just a vulnerable, naïve kid at the time. So, that gives me the strength to tell my story, so others who have felt the same "shame" will know that it shouldn't be their shame, but just a part of the abuse that they didn't cause. **And being brave is so much better than being scared.**

The war against abuse can only be stopped one person at a time. NOW IS THE TIME!

No More

No more silence
No more manipulation
No more secrets
No more pain
No more suffering
No more misery
No more lies
No more tears
No more hidden memories
No more future offenders
No more young lives changed forever
No more families destroyed
No more!

Chapter 31

They used our love against us

The family members in our lives who have hurt us have found a way to use our love against us. Like from the movie "The Green Mile" where the two little girls were being taken by a paedophile and were both told "If you scream, I'll kill your sister!" So, they both kept quiet instead of alerting their parents, as they didn't want their sister, whom they loved, to be hurt. If only they had screamed, they would still be alive. But they were manipulated into keeping quiet due to their love for one another. In this movie, the character John Coffey says, "I'm tired of people being ugly to each other." "I'm tired of all the pain I feel and hear in the world every day!" And I'm tired too, John, tired of hearing so many stories of suffering.

Similarly, our abusers have used our love for them against us. Who we thought loved us and what we thought was love was instead manipulation and abuse. But we kept quiet because we were dominated and lied to. They did this to keep us from getting help for ourselves. So instead, we were hurt time and time again because we were children and didn't know any better. Our abusers were the people we loved, looked up to and identified trust with at the time.

My perpetrator was nice to me at times when I was little and made me feel like they cared about me as their family member. But now I'm not so sure. I feel it was probably just manipulation. When they thought I was pulling away or were afraid I would tell someone what they were doing to me, they would use threats and coercive control to keep me quiet and continue their domination over me. So even after they stop abusing you, they still need to keep you quiet. So, the manipulation and control will then take on another form. Probably putting you down, making you feel shame or turning others against you with lies. Even trying to convince you that you participated willingly, anything so you won't speak up.

Childhood sexual abuse is like a double-edged sword. Trust and fear. So, at some point, the person you trusted turns into the person you then fear. And the fear also comes from the shame you feel inside about someone finding out what happened. But by now, I'm hoping you will fully understand this shouldn't be your shame. **We need to stop letting what happened to us define us as people.**

So, my abuser sexualised me from a very young age for their sick pleasure. Then, a few years later, they spied on me and humiliated me when they caught me doing something very private and personal that all kids do. And to add insult to injury, my abuser then threatened to tell kids at my primary school. This made me even more terrified of them and the humiliation of what may happen. (That fear I speak about). They didn't end up going through with their threat (as far as I know) but just the thought of this was so overwhelming and damaging to me. This is how they kept me quiet and continued their control of me. Therefore, I became an anxious, nervous, vulnerable, people-pleasing and self-doubting person.

This led to a lifetime of shame around sex and not feeling safe or being able to fully trust future partners.

When I was an adolescent, I had my supposed protector constantly drumming into me not to have sex before marriage, because this was the custom of their generation. This was so confusing to me, seeing as I had been sexualised as a child in the family home.

When I had my first long-term boyfriend, I was so damaged mentally and emotionally that I couldn't permit him to have sex with me. He would ask me, and I eventually told him, don't ask me, just do it. How sad is that? But because I was so scared of my supposed protector's reaction if they found out, I couldn't find a way to move past this self-doubt and guilt of going against their wishes. And having no confidence to make my own decisions, with their words constantly in my head. Another element from my childhood abuse and not knowing my own mind or being able to make big decisions throughout my teenage years. At the time, I struggled to know who I was, or what was right or wrong.

I recently heard about another childhood sexual abuse victim being abused by their own father. Then their father put guilt on them and said that if they told anyone, he would have to leave, and there would be no money for the family. This is the kind of mind-damaging/altering thoughts and guilt that abuse victims are faced with as children. This kind of manipulation is so detrimental to a child's thought processes and growth.

I found out a few years ago that my abuser not only did things to me but also another of our family members when she was a child.

Also, when I was about 15 years old, my abuser did stuff in secret to my vulnerable friend, who was two years younger than me. Which I wasn't told about until years later.

Once again, this is what I mean by keeping the "sick secret" and how others will be hurt if we don't speak up. As I'm sure it wasn't just the 3 of us that were manipulated and abused by my abuser. How many other families would have had this happen when the abuse was covered up and kept quiet?

I do wonder what happened to my abuser to make them do what they did to me. I asked them once over the phone to see if something happened to them as a child. It was a few years before I stopped having contact with them. I had a lot of health issues, and I thought maybe I needed to have it out with them once and for all so I could stop pushing my feelings down. Which I thought may have been making me sick. They pretended not to know what I was talking about and then belittled the situation when they knew I wasn't going to let it go. I tried to work things out somehow, so as not to break the family apart. I have a good idea who may have abused them if they were abused. But it's just a guess.

Hand On Your Shoulder

You see the world, through your innocent eyes,
One of Gods' little angels, just in disguise.
Finding magic in places, adults long ago forgot,
All the time in the world, until it suddenly stopped.

Your senses now heightened, like a rabbit, aware,
At nighttime you whisper, another unheard prayer.
You wake with a start, something makes you turn cold,
There's a hand on your shoulder, you're suddenly old!

Like a jack rabbit, your eyes dart here and there,
Breathing shallower now, but does anyone care?
One day a small child, with not a care in the world,
Next day under the covers, in a ball you are curled.

Such a big secret to hide, for such a sweet soul,
You can't get back, what that monster just stole.
No more than a child, now you're feeling so old,
Again, that hand on your shoulder, your body turns cold.

At nighttime you dream, of your world before this,
Of rainbows and unicorns, and mum's sweet kiss.
Can't she see that you've changed, no longer a child,
Do you hide it so well, when pretending to smile.

You've grown quieter now, than ever before,
Pleading don't leave, when mum walks out the door.
Don't want to go to school, just want to hold on to mum,
Unable to understand why, and feeling so numb.

But, mum never found out, and you never told,
Couldn't quite find the words, they had such a hold.
So you went through your life, this secret held tight,
Always hoping one day, you'd find the strength to fight.

One night, you dream you are older, standing so tall,
There's a ruckus outside, shadows cast on the wall.
You wake with a start, someone's walked in your room,
It's my monster again; your mind always assumes.

There's a hand on your shoulder, but not the same one,
Your prayers have been answered; there's no need to run.
You took a lifetime to find you, but you're finally bolder,
That gentle hand on your shoulder, is you, when you're older.

Chapter 32
You can bid the mob good day

"Man from Snowy River" movie reference here. There is a scene in The Man From Snowy River where the bushmen try to round up the wild brumbies. The horses head down a very steep mountainside, and all the riders stop, except for young Jim and his mountain brumby. They keep going after the wild brumbies because they know the terrain and can handle it.

This is where you will find out just who is in your circle of wagons. Who is strong and confident enough to stand with you and handle the terrain.

Charity is a coat you wear twice a year. It's kind of how I've felt when I've been trying to raise funds and awareness for a child abuse protection organisation. Not only raising funds for other children who have been abused and to educate parents to stop their children from being abused, but by telling my own story on their website, to hopefully open up a dialogue for adult survivors to speak up and receive help. It is so hard to get people to listen and care, let alone understand how a person's life is changed forever, because of what happened to them as a child. Sure, they may give money once or twice a year if you push them, **but how loud do you have to yell to get people to truly understand how this affects us all in one way or another?**

What I mean by being affected in one way or another, I spell out back in Chapter 12 – The Ongoing Hurt. Child sexual abuse may not have directly happened to you, but in some way, you may have been affected even if you don't know it at the time. You may see these people clearer now for who they really are, and not always in a bad way, but just realising how the people you've had in your life may have had something happen to them too.

Looking back, you may remember that person who road raged you for no real reason. That workmate who was always abrupt and had the "get you before you get me" attitude. Or that thoughtful friend who never forgot your birthday and always agreed with whatever you wanted to do. "The people pleaser." That person you saw as a tough guy with all the tattoos, but whose heart was as big as Texas. These people have struggled, whether it made them harder or softer, angrier or kinder.

I see people cringe all the time, change the subject and look embarrassed if I bring up childhood sexual abuse. These are the kind of people who will scroll past my social media posts. I can just imagine what they are thinking. Oh, there goes Deb bringing up "that subject" again. But some people will always make me feel heard, and these are my people. The ones who I can rely on. The ones who truly understand and can handle the terrain.

Some family members have always stood by me, but I've found a lot of great friends also, who have now become my family. My circle of wagons, again.

I gave a draft of this book to one of my best friends to read over. After reading it, she said "Deb, what could I have done to better support you over the years?" She is already such a caring, supportive friend. But it got me thinking. I think once you know someone has been through something like this, you should just make sure they know you are available to listen and support them when necessary. Check with them if they are okay with you asking how they are going at different times. Or whether they would prefer you not to bring it up unless they do.

I also remember writing a poem quite a few years ago about not forgiving my perpetrator and posting it on social media. Then I saw someone have a negative reaction to my post. I was a bit taken aback at first. But then, a few years later, I realised that they may have had similar circumstances happen to them also, so then I understood their reaction. They weren't offended by my post, but it had triggered them. So once again, I came to realise everyone is so different in their trauma responses and reactions.

So, some people may initially pull away from you when you speak your truth. Since this is not a nice subject or taboo, they may still be processing it. But just wait and see who comes back to you at a later date. Once they have had time to digest things or become braver themselves, then you'll be the one they have to thank for shining a light on the dark place they had been hiding in.

You may also be the person they can finally divulge the struggles they may be having due to one of their family members being abused and not knowing how to handle things.

Most importantly, be kind to yourself and keep remembering this was not your fault in any way. It is also not your fault if your family is broken. **That blame sits solely at your perpetrator's feet.**

As Billy Joel's song says – **We didn't start the fire!**

Take comfort in the fact, that we didn't start the fire!

Stuck

You are you,
And I am me,
But I'm not who,
I used to be.

I can't go back to where I was,
And you won't try, just because

So how can we get back to us?
If you are you and I am me.

The old ones stays and will not budge,
The young one grows but holds a grudge.

When wisdom doesn't come with age,
Just holding fast and don't engage,
The younger one becomes the wise,
These lessons learnt from open eyes.

Unto the grave, we hold our ground,
And never speak, or make a sound,
Though both are silently in grief,
And neither will find their relief.

But you are you,
And I am me,
I'm still not who I used to be.

But there are days when I get weak,
To break the silence, should I speak?
But what's the point, I can't go back,
To where I was, it's just too black.

So due to them, we stay apart,
You'll always be here in my heart,
But you are you,
And I am me,
Now, we're both not who we used to be.

Chapter 33

The only way out is through

Give me your hand, I will help you get through. One day at a time, we have so much to do!

We all, as child abuse survivors need to work through our trauma and make sense of what we've been through and who we are. As best we can.

If we don't work through our trauma, it will work its way through us!

Writing this book has triggered a lot of awful feelings and memories for me. But you must work through your trauma and grief. Otherwise, you'll never get healthier, mentally or physically. **It won't be silenced!** You have to do the hard work to get there, and it will be hard work, but it's better than where you are now. Believe me!

Trigger – meaning – to initiate, actuate or set off.

Other words for trigger are - bring about, cause, generate, produce, prompt, provoke and spark.

Triggering Warning – I see these words used a lot on social media, TV and other platforms. The preface to a traumatic story about to be told. But I do wonder if the people who need to hear something to move through their trauma are missing important information and details because they choose not to read or listen to it. **I personally don't think we can get to the other side without feeling our way through**. If we don't deal with or learn from circumstances similar to what we've been through. How are we ever going to be able to get stronger? These are just my thoughts and how I have dealt with my trauma, and of course, everyone should get guidance from their own professionals.

If you feel like you are reading a book written by different people. Well, you are. There is the confident person I have become from pulling away from my perpetrator and educating myself about my abuse. But most importantly I have finally found resilience and truth from writing about my experience. Also, how I've come to realise the family dynamics around intra-familial sexual abuse.

Then there is the little girl still wanting her supposed protector's protection and validation for what happened to her. To feel like she was important enough to be put first and not to have her pain hidden, to cover for her abuser's unnatural acts.

There is also the angry volcano in me, just waiting to erupt! Like a pressure cooker that sits just below the surface, ready to boil over at any time. Especially when I have so many people continuously coming up to me telling me about their own abuse stories. I am not saying that I don't want to help. Just the opposite. **But it just makes me so angry that this kind of hidden abuse is EVERYWHERE!**

Or I hear about another instance of child abuse happening right now and how I ache for that child's future self. Having to live through their own trauma experience and journey.

Then there is the person who still doubts herself even while writing this book. Continually wondering whether anyone will even be interested in reading it. Or whether it's any good? These thoughts never go away. They are still a small part of me.

But then there are also good things that have come from me dealing with my trauma, such as empathy. Being able to spot and understand other people's overreactions and trauma responses. Being strong enough to admit what happened to me, stand up for others, in similar situations and try to help them too.

My friend from childhood recently told me that after I stood up to her abuser, she finally got the strength to stand up to him also. This made me feel so proud that I had made such a difference to her when everyone else was letting her down. I would do it again in a heartbeat, too. I wish I could have done more for her, but I was just a kid. What she may not realise is that she helped me also. **By her being brave and telling me her story, I was finally able to reveal to her years later about my abuse.**

One thing I want to make very clear is that in no way am I looking for pity when I speak or write about my childhood abuse. I don't personally need to hear that someone feels sorry for me. More than anything I want people who've read my book to say how much it's helped them move forward. Or that their family member opened up about their struggles after reading my book. How the words they read in my book, they've felt the same way their whole lives, but couldn't make sense of their feelings, until now. Or how they've finally put themselves first and pulled away from family members who've tried to keep them down or silenced them.

I am also looking for knowledge, openness and an end to the silence for survivors. An understanding of what survivors endure throughout their lives. I want people to ask questions and educate themselves about this subject. TALK ABOUT IT!

To stop the ignorance, shame and harm from the silence, that has gone hand in hand with this subject in past generations.

This might not be the story anyone really wants to read. **But sure as shit, no one ever wanted to live it either.**

For me, writing this book has been my passion, but it is also a kind of compulsion. And, of course, I am very devoted to this cause. But I have also just had so many thoughts continuously swirling around in my head that there was no way to quiet them other than to write them down.

Poetry and songs

The poems I have written throughout this book have permitted me to express my emotions in a different format, which has been very liberating for me, and I hope others can relate to also. One of my poems has already been turned into a song by a talented friend.

People all over the world have turned to poetry in good times but also in times of grief or hardship. Or just when they needed to put their own life into some kind of perspective or tell a story.

Poetry and songs are a wonderful way to feel connected to others who have been through similar events in their life. Hearing the right words in a poem or song can make you feel that someone else has just explained your pain or turmoil, where you may not have been able to find the exact words yourself. Knowing you are not the only one who feels this way can make you feel connected to others when you may have felt alone previously. It can feel like someone has reached out to you in a special way to show you that you have this shared experience, and so you are less alone in your grief or trauma than you thought. A stranger who gets just how you feel and can pick you up in an unexpected but touching way.

I realise this may seem unusual, but my poem in Chapter 26, "You don't want to be me," which, by the way, is the one I'm the proudest of. I wrote in approximately 3 hours. It just came to me one morning and wouldn't leave me alone until I'd finished it. I had originally named it "Carnival comes to town" but after I wrote the line, "You don't want to be me" I felt this encapsulated the poem so much better.

For those of you who may not understand it entirely, it showcases my whole book in a really theatrical kind of layout. It talks about how all the people in the carnival are the people in our lives who have abused us or kept things hidden away. So, I will explain some of the poem's more important points below.

- **No money is needed, but there's always a fee** – explains that even though the kids are getting in free, they will pay in another way. Paedophiles will use tricks and presents, etc., to lure kids into bad situations by pretence.

- **The poster's now blank so she tries to turn back** – with this, I am trying to explain how Susie realises she has been tricked and wants desperately to leave the situation.
- **Bearded lady who hides her secrets so well** – one of the females in the family who keeps abuse hidden.
- **The knife thrower – no don't turn your back** – explains the family members who attack the survivor's character to keep the secrets hidden.
- **The bystander, who will just never speak** – once again, another family member who won't speak up and looks the other way instead of helping the victim.
- **The geriatric Nay Sayers** – are the older generations who have always denied the abuse was happening.
- **The extended family of the deaf, dumb and blind** – are the relatives who plug their ears, don't speak and close their eyes to the abuse happening all around them.
- **They see glitter and glamour, a sight to behold** – this is the façade abusers create to mesmerise young kids so they don't see the horrible truth.
- **To her friends, she says stop! You don't want to be me** – this is the most powerful line in the whole poem, and as I mentioned, the reason it became the title. Little Susie is desperately trying to stop her friends from going through the abuse that she herself has experienced.
- **They see now she's grown very strong from her scars** – this is so telling; Susie has gotten stronger because of what she's been through, understands and can now help others.
- **For 100's of years we've kept this secret padlocked** – explains how long this kind of abuse has been kept hidden, under lock and key, and therefore cycled again and again down throughout the generations.

- **The monsters on stage are still wearing their masks** – the perpetrators are walking amongst us as your average person, even family members.
- **The trauma in Susie is making her freeze** – this shows how our abuse can have such a negative effect on us that we will freeze in similar situations, especially as kids – a typical trauma response. Fight, flight or freeze.
- **Susie removes mum's rose-coloured glasses to see** - so many parents can be blind to the abuse that's going on right in front of them, or in their own home or deny it later as they can't or don't want to deal with it.
- **Susie's strength in herself has finally set her mum free** – Susie showing her mum the truth through her own strength, has made her mum finally realise what's been going on.
- **It's okay now mum, I've brought them out of the dark** – Susie has finally shown everyone who the perpetrators really are by exposing them and therefore, stopping the other kids from being abused.
- **But the journey from here mum, I must alone embark** – this line is sad but true. This is where Susie is telling her mum that it's her mental health and journey of recovery from here on and that Susie can only do this for herself.
- **And this generational story, can at last be unwrapped** – at last unwrapping this horrible secret for all to finally see and understand.
- **One monster unseen slips out through the tent's siding** – the unfortunate truth that this will always continue.

BUT WE CAN HELP STOP SOME OF IT! BY STANDING UP AND SPEAKING OUT!

I feel poetry has allowed me to dive deeper into my emotions and I think writing the poems is what I have enjoyed the most throughout this whole process. Anyone can write a poem, even if you have not been much of a writer before. Write how you feel. It doesn't even have to rhyme. Just put the words down and see how you go. It may help you release some strong emotions which can be very cathartic and healing.

I feel everyone is born with a talent. I remember watching Tinkerbell with my daughter when she was little and seeing her struggle to work out which talent was hers. She tried a lot of things before she realised what it was. To be a Tinker. A person who mends pans and other metal utensils. I feel now that I have also found my talent in a way, and it's taken me 50 years to discover this. I have previously written grants for community organisations, but never anything of this calibre. And you can clearly see why I've doubted myself after reading about my past. So, it is never too late to find your passion or talent, sometimes we can even find our potential through pain. At times, you are led to it kicking and screaming. But you will eventually find it if you keep an open mind and heart.

This is not a nice subject! But it is everywhere and, unfortunately, not going away anytime soon. Especially when it remains hidden. But a bright light needs to be shone on intra-familial childhood sexual abuse and childhood sexual abuse in general, because when we keep quiet and try to sweep it under the rug, as in generations before us, **this shit keeps happening, people!** We need to learn what not to do from past generations' mistakes.

I genuinely hope what I've written about in this book will give everyone a fair idea of how to do that.

I read an article somewhere that said there has not been an inquiry into "Intra-familial Sexual Assault." I, for one, want to know why. As mentioned in the article – Quote – **"These kinds of assaults are the most pervasive, soul-destroying and developmentally disaffecting types of crime that could ever be brought on a child"** – Unquote.

Sibling abuse is the most common form of intra-familial sexual assault.

So, moving forward, this is something I personally would like to see looked into, and I would be happy to help in any way.

To forgive or not to forgive? That is the question.

But what about forgiveness? Should you forgive the person who did this to you, and will this help you get through your hurt any quicker? I think this is only a question you can answer for yourself, and forgiveness can come in a lot of forms. It can be by releasing the person and any negative thoughts from your mind. Accepting them back into your life with grace and understanding. Moving forward positively and helping others to move forward. But it very much depends on your particular circumstances and how they have acted towards you later in life, to truly forgive them. Especially if there was an admittance and apology. That makes a big difference for forgiveness to come easier.

Then, there is the question of whether your abuser was abused as a child. It's a tough one, that's for sure. I think you need to deal with you, and they need to deal with them. They need to get help, especially if they are still offending. In this day and age, they must know it is wrong. And if they can't control themselves, they should seek psychological and medical intervention. Perhaps (chemical castration) if necessary to do this.

I feel that a good way to make perpetrators understand the damage they have done would be by making them listen to another victim/survivor (not their family member) tell their story and to let them know how damaging the abuse they were subjected to was. So basically, having an abuser listen to another victim, because then the emotion of hurt and revenge, etc., is taken out of the equation. That way, the perpetrator can also listen without being defensive, as they didn't harm this victim personally. Similar to hearing a victim impact statement by a different victim.

I tried to tell myself years ago that I forgave my abuser just so I could get through each day.

But it wasn't true for me back then as I realised you can't forgive someone who hasn't admitted to what they did, said they are sorry and asked what they can do to make things right. The pain this person has caused me regarding my dad's last year of life, I also can't forgive.

So, I have not waited for them to acknowledge what they did to heal myself. I am not interested in any punishment towards my abuser. My journey has been one of finally finding peace, and my "forgiveness currency" is to help others find their peace.

If anything, I feel pity for my abuser. They have had to live with themselves and what they've done, not just to me. But I do hope that they have tried to turn their life around for the people who are still around them and do some good moving forward. To try to make up for the wrongs they did when they were younger. **I hope they can one day admit how their actions have changed a life forever, because admitting is the first step towards moving forward for everyone.**

I have had a few people say to me that if you don't forgive your abuser, you are the one who won't heal as you carry this heavy burden around with you all the time. But I feel that I am healing by doing this work. Also, a conversation I heard from Dr Phil recently made a lot of sense to me. He said to a woman and her daughter who had both been abused by the woman's stepfather. You'll never truly get over what happened to you. **But you need to take your power back, and**

you do this by not letting your abuser control you from afar. So just like I keep saying throughout my book – we need to take that power back that was taken from us as children, and moving forward in a healthy way is paramount to being successful in doing that.

Then I found you that day, girl I should have been.

Through the hurt and the pain, you'll finally be seen

Chapter 34

You've always had the power, my dear......

The famous line from the end of The Wizard of Oz. **"You've always had the power my dear, you just had to learn it for yourself."** This is when the good witch Glinda tells Dorothy how to click the heels of her ruby slippers together three times. To get taken back home.

Just like in that iconic line from the movie. You have also had the power all along, too. You just didn't realise it.

One thing our abusers don't take into account is that their victims will grow up one day and become adults, too. **WE WILL REMEMBER** what you did to us. We may be fractured, but we are not broken. We can become stronger because of our struggles, and we will retake our power.

Our abusers are quite ignorant in this matter at the time of our abuse. That's why later on they need to inject toxicity into our lives, so they can protect themselves, as we grow older.

I, myself, have struggled to verbalise to my supposed protector just how my abuse has affected me. At times, it was due to their uneducated response, which led to an overly emotional reaction from me. That good old overreaction that is triggered within us. And in the end, they've gotten nowhere closer to understanding my pain.

I told you I thought I was no one of much importance at the start of my book. But who am I now in closing? I am every little boy or girl who has ever been abused. I am everyone who has had to live through their trauma. But I am as close to the "me" that I should have been, and I am FINALLY standing tall!

So you don't also have to struggle to verbalise your truth. I have purposely left lined pages at the end of this book. So you can write your own story and give it to the people YOU need to hear it. Hopefully when they get to the end of my book and then read your story. They will be able to better understand how you feel and how to help you.

Be brave and speak from the heart xx

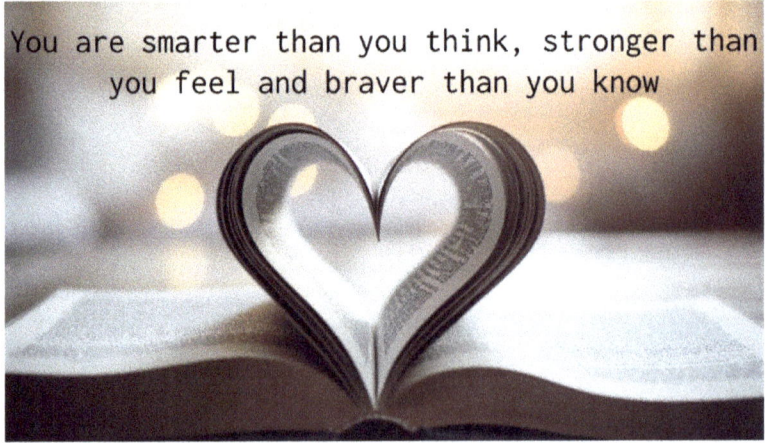

Do you hear me now

It's been a long, tough, winding road,
At times you've drifted in - uninvited,
My mind wasn't strong, and it showed,
And this poor creature you thought benighted.

I cried out for help in my soul,
Can't anyone hear my request?
Man, your heart must be so hollow,
Empty as a tin man's chest.

On a dusty windblown hill,
My mind would wander and sit,
Felt like time grew sightless and still,
Never knew silence quite like it.

Domination their double-edged tool,
Never was a level playing field,
In life's pantomime, we played the fool,
Left broken, pain rarely revealed.

With a mind like delicate china,
Sensitivity, your Achilles heel,
Bastards always had a way to find ya,
Anguish too great to ever reveal.

For those of you who couldn't hold on,
In that river where they drowned you,
You'd see that you were never alone,
We're all here now, love surrounds you.

Do you think they'll hear me now?
I can't yell any louder than this,
Broadcast it if I knew how,
No longer their tale to dismiss.

Chapter 35

Give me your hand, so I can push you back down

This was the chapter that I never knew I'd write. It's about what happened after finishing the draft of my book.

I have struggled throughout writing this book about what reaction my supposed protector would have when they found out about this book. Also, the fact that I wanted to advocate for other survivors. Because I was always looked upon as the good girl in the family growing up and conditioned to not say anything about my abuse, but now in some bizarre way, I have become the villain instead of the victim in this situation for speaking out to a potentially large audience.

So....... here is the chapter that wasn't meant to be written. But it may well be one of the most important chapters in this whole book.

As I said, I have been struggling and stressing about how writing this book will affect my supposed protector. Therefore, I had gently pulled away from them for the last year or so. I was also trying to help someone close to me get away from their abuser and bystander, which also made it very hard for me to want to be around my supposed protector. When they called or texted, I'd get a tight feeling in my chest and have to take some deep breaths before responding to them. To be fair, they had no idea I was writing a book or that I'd pulled away. But during this time, I also realised that our relationship was all very surface and not much depth. There wasn't much contact coming from them to me, either. I couldn't talk to my supposed protector about the most important work I had done in my whole life. Or how confident and proud I felt about myself and that I felt ready and able to help others now.

While writing this, there is a sadness in me, but there is also a new strength from finally being free from my inner turmoil. The image I had built up in my head about this person as a child has finally been put to rest. Once and for all. **That little girl's dream of who she thought this person was to her and what she thought she had is gone.**

I had been confiding in family and close friends about my constant struggles to reconcile my thoughts and feelings about this. Also not knowing how to move forward with my supposed protector. I had, for the most part, been told "You'll probably never get what you want from this person, Deb." I kept arguing and saying, but they are not dumb, they have always stood up and been assertive during their life at other times! Why can't they now listen, understand and stand up for me and other survivors? It all didn't make sense in my brain as I thought I knew them best, as I had known them my whole life. But I am obviously a slow learner and have to always find out things the hard way.

So, the conversation didn't start great, with them realising where this was heading and telling me that they didn't want to talk about "that."

Because of their response, we talked about our relationship. I told them I don't feel close to them because they have never made themself available to talk to me or help me with my abuse trauma. I let them know that I feel we have a very superficial relationship. As in, we never get into anything significant to me due to them not wanting to hear what happened. I also needed to talk to them about some other stuff going on with another person and their abuse of people close to us both. I told them I felt I had been left to dangle in the wind and fix myself my whole life.

As I have said many times before, it may not be a nice subject to talk about, what we survivors have been through. But we have had to live with it our whole lives, and how does anyone think that feels?

To their credit, they finally agreed to sit down and talk to me. Most of the conversation went well, with them asking questions for the first time, and they also seemed to be listening. I won't get into any particular details, but the talk seemed to be heading in the right direction for some healing to finally occur.

I felt they were finally being honest with me, too. We hugged and cried at times, and I was starting to feel there was a chance to move forward.

That was until I told them I wanted to help other survivors who have gone through what I have been through now, too. That's when the wall came back up.

I was asked how I was going to help other survivors. I mentioned a social media post I had put up a while ago with my outrage about a child abuse situation I'd seen recently on the news. I told my supposed protector that in my social media post, I put forward the question "If you don't think you know of any child abuse survivors, well, you're listening to one now."

Then I told them that I wanted to be an advocate to help others, and I had just written a book. From one survivor to another. And that's when everything really went south!

I was told that I couldn't write a book. I responded, "But I already have."

They then told me that you're not an expert or counsellor. I explained to them that I realised that, but I now have a lot of life experience and knowledge in this area because I've lived it and seen it my whole life, I know just what it feels like to go through it personally.

By now, I am starting to feel they are trying to question my worth and intelligence.

They then told me "No, there are plenty of books out there already. They don't need yours." This was quite absurd coming from someone who'd never educated themselves about this subject.

I told them once again I had written my book and was going to publish it.

They then told me that publishing my book would destroy them! Meaning my abuser and their family.

I let them know in no uncertain terms that I am doing this for me and other survivors. Not to hurt anyone, and I've not named my abuser once throughout my book. I have every right to express how I feel and how this has affected my whole life. Especially as it will help so many others, and that's the most important thing.

And while we are on the topic of destroying people, **I told them that what my abuser did to me as a little girl has destroyed my**

childhood, family relationships, and so much more. So, let's not go there!

It is amazing to me how much silencing, gaslighting, and victim shaming/blaming goes on in these intra-familial abuse circumstances, especially to try to keep us silent and the secret tightly locked away.

And that's when they left. But instead of crying or feeling guilty, I was proud that I didn't cave again to the pressure I had felt my whole life to be silent. But what I felt was relief. Just relief, that they had finally given me the answer I needed to let go and move forward at last.

Knowing for certain that the secret and their alliance with my abuser had and will always be their priority. A thing I had always felt but, until now, not had confirmation of.

The ironic thing is that if my abuser had just admitted to what they did to me and apologised, I was willing to go to family counselling to try to work through this and keep our family together. But they didn't.

Another great example of the irony of this situation is that if my supposed protector had held my abuser to account, just once and not silenced me my whole life and had tried to help me work through my trauma, you wouldn't be reading this now. I hate to have to say it again. **But just like the name of this book – "Circling the wagons" around the perpetrator and not the victim is why I am here now.**

So, just like the saying "What we fear we create" rings so true in this circumstance. Due to both of them not doing the right and moral thing, it has now led to this book being written. **I don't feel any blame at all, and never again will I feel any shame.**

If parents don't hold their children accountable during their lives, the child thinks there are no consequences for their actions. They are disabling their children, and the lesson that person will finally learn may be the hardest of all. And this goes for wives or other family members who don't hold an abuser, such as a husband, to account. They will learn the hard way the consequences of their inaction.

You would think my supposed protector would want me to be a strong woman and help other survivors be strong. But they obviously don't. Because they think it will be at the expense of my abuser and the "secret." Irrespective of whether this has been brought on by guilt or something else and whether they want to admit it or not, this has always been more important than me. I was hoping that if I pulled away, maybe they would change their mind, miss me and not want to lose me. But I suppose you can't change teams in the 4th quarter because the narrative they've told themselves for decades is too ingrained in them.

Once again, I have lost another person due to my past abusive situation. But I suppose you can't lose what you never really had.

So, I will end by saying this. Finding out the truth about your family members will be hard, **but you can't truly be you until you do!**

A saying I found recently may also help if, at times, you struggle as I have in the past –

You can borrow my belief in you until you find yours again – unknown.

This is the end of my story, but hopefully only your beginning xx

Acknowledgements

Putting a book like this together doesn't happen overnight or without help, support and encouragement from a lot of very special people.

Unfortunately, I'm not able to name everyone individually, but if you were there for me, you know who you are!

I want to thank my son Mitch for his talented drawings throughout this book.

My husband, children and cousin, for encouraging me to find my voice to help others and showing me their love and support along the way.

All my wonderful friends for standing by me during the writing of this book and for their continued support of my healing throughout my journey.

I've been very fortunate to have the help of other authors during my writing experience. A process that was so foreign to me at times, that I had no idea what my next move was, especially around publishing my book.

So, I'd like to sincerely thank the following authors –

Rachel King, Natalie Kile, Nova Gibson and Megan Harris.

Testimonials

What a powerful message you're giving to survivors of all types of abuse! "This is not your secret, it's your story!" Shannon R

So many people will feel seen and heard with this book! Indi M

A raw, honest and courageous tale of a victim who used her trauma as power. It lights the path for others who suffered the often under-reported travesty of child abuse. This book reads as a warning to parents, a rebuke to offenders and a torch for the mistreated. It is a story of protected deviance and silenced victims. Well, one of those victims found her voice and thank god she did. Angela B

Deb was really able to capture the environment that is created for a child who is betrayed by people who are meant to protect them. We shouldn't look away from the reality and impact of child abuse. A thought-provoking read. Christine B

Testimonials

Deb is a wonderful example of how to take back your power and become stronger through self-discovery after experiencing the trauma of intra-familial abuse. This book helped me understand the importance of listening and being present for those needing support and brave enough to speak up. This is an extraordinary personal account of her journey and what has helped in her healing process. Monica F

Deb courageously steps into her truth to shine a light on Intra-familial Child Sexual Assault and the family systems that perpetuate and conceal it. It was a privilege to read it. Thank you Deb for being a voice for Survivors of IFCSA. Michelle H

I absolutely love the heartfelt sentiment and urgency of your message that so many people need to hear. I'm so sorry you had to go through this. Please put it out to the world, and never be discouraged. Your writing is fantastic, but your message is even more so. Nova G

Deborah has reclaimed her strength, courage, confidence and power in writing this book. I hope that by reading it, many others in a similar situation will be able to release guilt and self-blame and finally heal. Cynthia

What an honour to be trusted with your story Deb. Your journey has not defined you as a person, but one that will inspire others to reach out for help. The heart heals in many ways, Deb's courage will not only inspire others to stand up and be heard but hopefully let the healing begin. I am so proud of the person you are Deb. You are amazing. Donna P

I just sat and read your book cover-to-cover. At times I cried for the little girl whose innocent childhood was so horribly derailed and then for the protection she was denied, the protection she had every right to expect. But I also cried for the adult who has so bravely and determinedly smashed open the "dirty little secret" hidden by families for generations. For the adult who wants others to realise they are not alone. I am so sorry you were forced to endure that abuse and that your supposed protector failed you. But I am so proud of what you are doing. Jodie B

It is heartbreaking to imagine that we need a book such as Circling the Wagons. That society needs a guidebook on how to navigate intra-familial sexual abuse. Deb delivers a candid insight into the internal dialogue of the survivor, whilst gently offering understanding and hope for healing. I recommend this book to anyone who is looking for clarity when troubled by the behaviours of their loved ones or those who continue to ignore or coverup what has happened to them. Rachael K

Author Bio

Deb grew up in the 70's and 80's in Sydney, Australia.

This was a time of roaming the streets with the neighbourhood kids on bikes or roller skates, and time to go home was when it was getting dark. Our parents knew which house we were at by the bikes out on the front lawn and a "cooee" was enough to get our butt's home.

This was a time before stranger danger was known about. It was also a time when family sexual abuse was not widely known or talked about. A time when kids were left home alone from a young age and supervision was nowhere near what it is today.

Deb tried hard for years to block out what happened to her as a child, especially for her family's sake. She did this by always keeping busy and compartmentalising her life.

She went from one bad relationship to another and always felt like she wasn't good enough.

Raising a family and working kept these thoughts at bay for decades.

But her body finally gave way and started to show her that she couldn't keep her trauma down any longer.

After a substantial medical operation, she was forced to stop work for a period of time and realised just how exhausted she really was.

Author Bio

This gave her time to process her life and began her writing journey. A journey that felt forced upon her in a way, due to the abuse she saw all around her and wanting to help others find their voice by telling her own story.

She now advocates for other adult survivors and hopes this will be her continued path into the future with advocacy, public speaking and promoting changes to the way intra-familial abuse circumstances are dealt with.

Since publishing the first edition of *Circling The Wagons* in 2024, Deb has been honoured with numerous keynote speaking engagements, research collaborations, podcast features, presentations, and a webinar. She has travelled nationally, sharing her powerful storytelling and advocating for adult survivors of child abuse and promoting the importance of prevention.

Deb's unwavering commitment to supporting adult survivors, preventing child abuse through insights from her own lived experience, and educating the broader community, has established her as a vital voice in the movement for greater awareness and systemic change.

She also founded **dragonflyadvocacy.com.au** - a safe, anonymous space where survivors can access support through her ongoing blog posts or reach out to her directly after reading her book.

If *Circling The Wagons* has helped you, and you would like to support Deb in continuing her mission to uplift survivors and protect future generations, please consider:

- Leaving a review on any online book retailer's website
- Requesting the book at your local library, high school, or university

Every action helps strengthen this vital movement.

Some images in this book are designed by Freepik.com

Glossary

Abuse

Verb –
- use (something) to bad effect or for a bad purpose, misuse.
- Treat with cruelty or violence, especially regularly or repeatedly.

Noun –
- the improper use of something.
- cruel and violent treatment of a person or animal.

Trauma

Noun –
- a deeply distressing or disturbing experience.
- a disordered psychic or behavioural state resulting from severe mental or emotional stress or physical injury.

Paedophile
- a person who is sexually attracted to children.

Perpetrator
- a person who carries out a harmful, illegal or immoral act.

Manipulation
- the act of manipulating someone in a clever or unscrupulous way.

- an attempt to sway someone's emotions to get them to act or feel a certain way.

Intra-familial Abuse
- sexual abuse that occurs within the family.
- family members - involves a child in (or exposes a child to) sexual behaviours or activities.

Family Member
- a parent, child, sibling, aunt, uncle, cousin or grandparent.

Mental Illness
- a condition that causes serious disorder in a person's behaviour or thinking.

Supposed Protector
- Supposed – generally assumed or believed to be the case, but not necessarily so.
- Protector - a person or thing that protects someone or something.

www.ingramcontent.com/pod-product-compliance
Lightning Source LLC
Chambersburg PA
CBHW062057290426
44110CB00022B/2624